Behold the Glory

Other Books by the Same Author

•

POETRY

EDEN TWO-WAY
THE FACTUAL DARK

•

SOCIAL THEORY

EARLY CHRISTIANS OF THE 21ST CENTURY

•

BASIC THEOLOGY

STOP LOOKING AND LISTEN
CAMPUS GODS ON TRIAL

•

LITERARY CRITICISM

C. S. LEWIS: APOSTLE TO THE SKEPTICS

•

FOR CHILDREN

KNOCK AND ENTER

•

Chad Walsh

Behold the Glory

H | B

Harper & Brothers, New York

WGE

The following chapters appeared in *Episcopal Churchnews:* November 27, 1955, "A Tomato in the Autumn Sun"; December 11, 1955, "The Bowing Order"; December 25, 1955, "Basic Training for the Love of God."

For

Harry and Virginia Wolfe

Contents

[vii]

Jesus saith, Wheresoever there are two, they are not without God: and where there is one alone I say I am with him. Lift up the stone and there shalt thou find me: cleave the wood, and I am there.

—*Oxyrhynchus Papyrus* 1

PART ONE

Double Vision

Hints, Goads, and Lures

I CANNOT remember what city it was, and the very name of the church has slipped me. Only one thing from that Sunday remains in my mind. The time was almost 10:45, and I was standing in a side room with the choir, waiting for the organist's signal. The sermon I intended to give was one I had preached several times before. My mind, in the minute or so that remained before the procession, was free to wander aimlessly.

It always gives me an odd feeling to be with a group of people whom I am not likely to meet again. Something of this thought was in the back of my mind as I glanced about and began studying the faces of the choir members. What I saw did not make me hope that the future would bring us all back together. They were a singularly unattractive group of men and women. Their lack of appeal to the eye was not merely a physical thing, though the men inclined toward premature paunches, and the women were either fat or had the

Grant Wood look of American Gothic and sour repression. It was more the blankness of their faces.

My mind dallied with the paradox. What a drab crew this was—and yet it would shortly be hard at work, singing praises to the God of joy and exaltation. Strange heralds of glory they were.

I continued watching the choir members, and I felt quite apart from them. I had no sense that we were fellow pilgrims of eternity; it was more as though I were inside a house, ironically observing the absurdities of life down the street. To pass the time, I mentally tried to put into words the paradox of these drab singers making a joyful noise unto the Lord. If I could phrase it cleverly, it would amuse my friends back home.

If this should seem an odd state of mind for someone soon to enter the pulpit, I grant it. And indeed, the recounting of the experience is more than a little embarrassing. I should gladly pass it by in silence except that I must set the stage for what follows.

As I say, I was standing there with the choir, thinking these ironic thoughts, and trying to find witty words for them. "Gargoyles," I suddenly said to myself. These shapeless or misshapen faces were like the gargoyles that every tourist in Paris feels obligated to photograph from the roof of Notre Dame. My mood of ironic detachment grew stronger. The organist had still not given his signal. "Gargoyles," I repeated to myself, so that I should not forget the apt word.

Then something happened. As I silently repeated the word once more, from nowhere came five additional words. "To the glory of God" I found myself adding, and the phrase was complete: "Gargoyles to the glory of God."

The new words were singing inside me with such frenzied joy and triumph that I did not stop to ask whence they came. Instead, I looked at the choir members again.

If I could go to sleep some night in a reasonably adequate hotel and wake up next morning in heaven, I do not think I should find greater changes. It was as though an alchemist had invisibly passed through the room and done his work of transmutation. Here were the faces, the faces I had studied with analytical detachment; but each now reflected a light or a light shone from each. It was not a light that has any ordinary source. But thanks to this light, I was able to see each face for the first time.

I was no longer surrounded by drab and transient mortals. These men and women were akin to gods and goddesses, not to gargoyles or mere human beings. Each face was more uniquely itself than before; each taught me that a master sculptor had lavished eternity on it, creating its planes, angles, and curves. I am saying this clumsily; it is almost impossible to communicate the thing. But the light on every face revealed such beauty, face by face, that it was almost more than I could do to let my eyes travel from one to the next.

These changes were great enough, but there was a greater. I was no longer studying these men and women; I was simply with them. I wonder now whether the same invisible light that made their faces live for me was also on my own face. At that time, I did not think to wonder. Here were these people; I was with them. The little bit of space that separated one of us from the other was as conventional and unreal as the line on a map dividing Wisconsin from Illinois. We were part of one another, we were part of the whole body of men and women—past, present, and future—who have met and will meet to preach inevitably inadequate sermons to the glory of God and sing lamentably inadequate praises to His holy Name. And it seemed to me that this was as it should be; that God must be smiling with approval at His gargoyles, who had come together to offer Him their poor best.

Now it is not true that we gargoyles had become

more pleasing to the impartial camera; even in the midst of my long moment of knowledge, I retained sufficient detachment to test this. The radiance that shone on or from each face did not cancel out the plainness, the downright ugliness, that would have been certified by the camera. But the ugliness had ceased to trouble me. It was engulfed by beauty of a kind that would be scarcely endurable if we had to look on it every waking minute.

I have no desire to argue with the camera; what it sees and records is there. But neither that Sunday morning nor afterward was I able to explain away the glory, the radiance, the beauty. It was so real, and is so living a part of my memory, that I could more easily call my own existence an illusion than deny this brief eternity of knowledge.

I now know—though it was long before I found any words for it—that we can see double. I know that the camera sees some things, but I know also that it does not see all things.

Whenever I think about my experience with the choir —and the actual time may not have been more than ten seconds, before the special vision began to fade—it seems mysteriously linked with other moments. One of them was near the beginning of World War II when I overcame my shameful horror of needles sufficiently to sign up with the Red Cross as a blood donor. With unwelcome promptness the office telephoned me to tell me of my day and hour. I still remember how I felt as I walked to the gymnasium, which had been converted into a barracks of temporary cots. I was disgusted at my cowardice and angry at my tense muscles and rebellious nerves. I was resolved to see this thing through if it killed me—which it probably almost would.

My tension and anger remained strong while I went through the preliminaries of registration; they were stronger yet when it came my turn to stretch out on a cot. At long last the nurse expertly—though not without causing a little pain—inserted an oversize needle into the inner side of my elbow. Then, almost immediately, I felt a deep calm. I suppose this was natural enough; the worst was over. But I have no simple explanation for what followed. It was not merely a lessening of tension; it was something positive rather than negative. I was plunged and drowned in "the peace that passeth all understanding." I lay on the cot in perfect contentment—but that is too lifeless a word. I had no thought of time—it had stopped. I had no past, no future, no desires. I looked across at the gray-haired man on the next cot. We did not speak, but we were united. I had a curious conviction that no man's blood belongs to himself; that today, as always, it was invisibly flowing from one body to another. This seemed obviously true, and the kind of truth that brings quiet joy.

After an age without time, time returned in the form of the nurse. She helped me up, led me to another room, pointed out fruit juice and sandwiches, and told me I could leave in fifteen minutes. But even as I walked home, my watch still seemed to be running very slowly.

I have since been a blood donor a number of times. My dislike of needles is as humiliating and intense as ever, but the sense of timelessness and human oneness has never returned to me on any other Red Cross cot. Evidently there is an element of grace about these moments. You cannot demand them; they simply come —sometimes.

Two more memories, and I am done with my confessions. The first is an experience from my early 'teens. I was roaming up a country road a mile or so from my home town of Marion, Virginia. When I came to the top of a small rise I looked across a field, and beyond it lay a woodland, filled with chestnut trees in flower. A few years later these trees were all to be blackened with blight, and dead. But at that time they were full of growing life; they rose tall and straight, and their branches were white like the froth of successive waves breaking on a shore. At least that is the way I would describe it now. At that time I had never seen the ocean, and I doubt that I tried to put anything into words. The mania for communicating the incommunicable came later.

In any case I sensed, as though I could touch and taste it a quarter of a mile away and feel it in my muscles, the surge of life racing up through the straight boles of the trees—racing to explode in a sea of wind-tossed white. Something stirred alive within me; the chestnut trees and I were linked by hidden roots across the intervening pasture.

My final memory is of a moment of knowledge that has recurred several times during the ten years I have taught at Beloit College. Ordinarily I walk across the campus and everything seems ordinary. The buildings are a familiar assortment of collegiate styles; the trees are the accustomed oaks, elms, and the like, of southern Wisconsin. I know the campus almost too well; I know each path by heart. They are useful, prosaic things; they can lead me to Middle College for my mail, or to the Union for a cup of coffee, or to Morse-Ingersoll Hall where my classes meet.

This is how the campus ordinarily appears to me.

But a few times—a very few—I have suddenly caught myself seeing it with new eyes, as though I were a visitor from another planet. The very trees take on the individuality of loved faces. It is obvious that they have been separately created, with exquisite attention to each detail of limb and leaf. I look at Middle College, the square brick building that was once the entire college, a little more than a hundred years ago. It looms before me, now heroic in size and stance. Here, visible to my eyes that are usually so dull, is a fortress of the human spirit, created brick by brick because a handful of far-seeing men were not content to let the frontier sink into the barbarism that was long a lively possibility.

And the paths. For a short while I see paths as they really are—the veins and arteries of social and intellectual relations between one human being and another. Thanks to the particular path, a well-worn one, which I am following, I can easily walk to the Union for a midmorning cup of coffee. While there, I strike up a conversation with several other professors and two or three students. It is a meeting at one of the way stations of eternity. Something is said that sets me thinking; some modification, however tiny, has been made in the total way I meet the world. And I look at the students, who

[21]

cannot hide their hunger—hunger for what?—anything I can give them? I know that ten or twenty years from now, for good or evil, one of them may be a fraction changed because of this half hour with me.

⇒ II ⇐

Emissaries from Somewhere

IT IS very difficult to write of these things; they are so intimate that it seems a desecration to set them down on paper. But I cannot believe that there is anything peculiar to me in these unnegotiated moments when a door briefly opens and as quickly closes.

Certainly, the arts all bear plain witness. The heavenly vistas of Dante's *Divine Comedy* grew from that luminous instant when, at the age of nine, he first beheld the eight-year-old Beatrice. Wordsworth's poetry again and again evokes his own memories of the opening door:

> There was a time when meadow, grove, and stream,
> The earth, and every common sight,
>   To me did seem
>   Apparelled in celestial light.*

* "Ode, Intimations of Immortality from Recollections of Early Childhood," quoted from *The Poetical Works of Wordsworth,* ed. Thomas Hutchinson, Oxford University Press, London, 1928, page 587.

Dante and Wordsworth are merely two of the more articulate explorers who have peered through a door long enough to record some recollections of what they saw inside.

Painters, sculptors, and composers bear identical witness, for anyone who consents to see or listen. But your friends are sufficient witnesses if you are willing to speak first. I have discovered that when one person overcomes his shyness enough to confess some moment of the quickly opening door, there is immediately a babble of eager conversation, as others match his experience. Deeply and urgently we want to share these moments—but only with those who will understand.

Let me turn the tables. I have made my confessions; have you nothing in your own memory that corresponds to them? Perhaps your experiences do not have the same immediate sources as mine. With many people, music is the most powerful catalyst. A friend told me of one day when she was listening to Beethoven's "Fifth," and for the first time became absolutely convinced of the existence of God—"it was a mounting feeling—everything fell into place because there is God." But almost anything can open a quick door into—something. It may be a glimpse of one face, a face you have never seen before, in a subway crowd. The skyline of a city, the sight of small green shoots where you had planted seeds, children jumping rope—one of these may at some time have been your magic key. Or your clearest moment of double seeing may come on a day of bitter renunciation, when nothing but a sober sense of duty compels you to a decision that violates every nerve in your body. Often the door opens in foxholes, in boats adrift on the ocean, in times of desperate illness; there seems no human state too serious or too trivial to be the immediate cause.

If you search your memory, I think you will find many instances of the quickly opening door; and you will half recall something beyond the door, though you cannot say exactly what it was.

But when the door opens, however briefly, what does this opening mean?

I shall start with this assumption: Common sense is not sensible if it finds no meaningful place for moments that are more real, while they last, than the eyes with which I look through the opening door, or the ears that seem to hear new music from behind the door. It may be that the door opens into a room, a house, a second universe meant for me. I must find out.

It is true that these moments of sudden insight add up in a long life to very few minutes of clock time; at least that is true for most of us. Plotted on a time-study chart, the moments would not seem worthy of a separate category. But it is quality of time that matters, not duration. Most of the hours of my life appear so empty in retrospect that I have not the slightest memory of what I was doing at 4:15 p.m. three days ago. It is the special moment that stands out in recollection, as one face at a party will haunt you after you have forgotten twenty other faces.

The moments of the opening door make up in intensity for what they lack in length. We must deal with them in one way or another. So far as I can see, there are three ways.

One way is to be a foot-loose quester and live for thrills, mystery, and secret knowledge. Such a person dwells greedily on each luminous experience vouchsafed to him; lives it and relives it in his imagination; sometimes aids his imagination by drink or drugs. He often roams the earth in search of some place where the door will stay open all the time. To an observer, his life may seem a succession of separate quests: a love affair, an exploring expedition, the frantic pursuit of some art, dabbling in strange religions. But this is merely the outer appearance. All his quests are part of one quest. He wants to force the door open, get inside, and stay there. He is convinced that once inside, he will be at home for the first time.

There are worse ways of spending a life. A philosophic drifter, moving from place to place and from experience to experience, may wear out but will not dry out. Still, he fails. The door cannot be battered open.

Society, reasonably seeking its own stability, encourages us to choose a second alternative—to disregard the door as much as possible, quickly forget its intrusive moments of opening, and in general go about our daily business. This way of life also has much to recommend it. The routine of earning a living, being a dutiful husband and parent, and rendering one's duty to community and country is not to be despised.

But being too completely at home in the commonwealth of common sense has its price. To measure the cost, attend the twentieth reunion of your college class. There you meet one of your classmates, still vigorous and well kept, and obviously prosperous. With him is his wife, also well kept. Their marriage is a secure one; they are sincerely dedicated to each other. But you remember when they first met. You recall the time he summoned courage to tell you about her, as though Adam were describing Eve to a visiting angel. The light of that first vision, in which he saw her as more than a mortal senior at the state university, has faded into a comfortable domestic glow. Perhaps it had to. But the loss is there.

There is loss, too, in your friend's vanished appreciation of poetry and music. You notice also that he no longer talks of a hiking trip some day through western Ireland, though he now has the money to make it possible. He has come to terms with life; he has prospered; he is a successful—and diminished—being. You go away, wondering whether he is thinking the same about you.

If it were a choice between being a foot-loose quester on the one hand, or a dutiful embodiment of common sense on the other, the human predicament would be desperate past the power of words to say. But God can count above two. Perhaps both extremes err, and equally. There may be a middle path, or possibly a third path, which is quite distinct from the other two.

Let us assume—and see where the assumption leads us—that a third possibility exists. Let us assume that the door that quickly opens and more quickly closes is intended to tease and goad us into asking questions and seeking answers. Let us assume that the fragmentary glimpses through the open door are meant to point beyond themselves, to something or somebody we have been destined from all eternity to meet. Finally, let us assume also that this sober inquiry can be pursued while we are still doing our daily duties and living in the midst of common sense; that we need not buy a ticket to any strange and distant place, but can remain where we are, concerned with our work and our families, and explore whatever is waiting to be explored.

Offhand, these fractional moments of double vision have the look of strangely dressed emissaries from a foreign and perhaps better land. I shall stay where I am, and at the same time follow the envoys wherever they lead me. Possibly they will conduct me to their country, and I shall be made a naturalized citizen there, so that I can freely move back and forth between two worlds.

⇶ III ⇜

When the Door Opens

WHEN the door suddenly swings open, for however brief a moment, the axioms of common sense stammer into silence. A non-Euclidian geometry of human experience has for the instant assumed command, and it possesses its own axioms.

As I think about it, I see that nearly every experience of the opening door has seven characteristics—or at least most of them:

(1) *You forget yourself.* The world no longer revolves around your desires, your hopes and fears and ambitions. You have a sense of liberation, as though you had escaped from a small, dark room. Perhaps one familiar word will sum it up: humility. You are surprised into humility. Or call it simply unselfconsciousness. Whatever the word, you are freed, if only for a split second, from the nagging self. This is so mighty an act of liberation that when you must again make terms with the

forgotten self, it is as though a runaway slave were being led back into servitude.

(2) *It is personal.* Perhaps this seems a contradiction. I said a moment ago that the self is forgotten, and now I am asserting that the experience is intensely personal. But there is actually no contradiction. A man does not become fully himself until he stops thinking about himself. It is the people who talk least of "self expression" who have the most to express; and it is they who can give themselves most freely, and most freely receive.

Your response to the quick eternities of double sight is more like falling in love than adjusting a microscope. In our daily lives, all of us are trained to be analytical observers, to study and mentally dissect whatever is before us—a river course, a problem, a human being. This habit of observation is useful and often necessary, but it is the examination of a dead world, a world in which even men and women are "objects" to be classified, not immortal companions to know and to love. In the luminous moments, all is reversed; the very trees and grass, the stones themselves, appear as living and perceiving beings. It is a face-to-face meeting: The "I" confronts the "thou." The whole of your being gladly greets the whole—of what? You greet it; you are not separate from it. It may be merely a tree in front of you.

No matter; the tree is in this moment more a living companion than are men and women during the times when you are the detached observer of the dead world.*

(3) *Time stops.* At their most intense, these instants are carriers of eternity, all time made accessible in the tick of a clock and thereby transcended. It is not a mere sterile timelessness, a cosmic stagnation, but rather the fullness of time. It is time summoned into a "now" that is not time, but that holds the wealth of all time. The moment when you first realize that you have fallen in love may serve as an example; but life is studded with these timeless times when eternity briefly plants its gay banner and establishes a beachhead among the clocks and calendars.

(4) *The splendor.* Whatever sights you see, whatever sounds you hear, whatever tastes you savor, it is as though your senses had been drugged until that moment. You afterward wonder whether this may not be a mercy. Could anyone constantly bear such a blazing brightness of sky and tree, the smell of hay in the fields, the taste of apples fresh from the tree, the distant cry of a sea gull? If every face had the radiance of this one face, would you dare walk in crowds?

* In this chapter and the next I am deeply indebted to Martin Buber's *I and Thou,* translated by Ronald Gregor Smith.

You begin to understand why an artist often seems to be intensifying and exaggerating what he depicts. Perhaps he is simply painting it as it is.

(5) *It points beyond itself.* The autumn hillside blazes with a color and light that no photograph can reproduce. And yet you know it is only an outpost; its splendor is a reflected splendor, as the moon gives back the earth's light. The greatest music is no more than the shorthand notes of special explorers, set down in haste so that the lands they have visited can be at least partly revealed to the people at home. Human love itself, even the most complete love of man and wife, points toward love that is more than mortal.

Every moment of splendor, every broken fragment of splendor, is a rumor of that splendor which is whole and constant. Each mystery affirms the final mystery that is at once the ground and illumination of all lesser mysteries, the goad and the goal of our searching.

(6) *It does not stay.* The moment comes when it will; it stays as long as it chooses; it departs at its own time, not yours. As soon as you begin clinging to it, pleading for it to linger, you have lost it. Your desperate ego is clamoring; the vision fades utterly. The moment is a gift of grace, unearned and unnegotiated.

(7) *It bequeaths understanding.* The moment goes,

but it leaves behind a memory, and—if you are willing—a new knowledge. Everything, seen in the memory of this brighter light, is caught in a dialogue between mere time and the fullness of time. Take the love of man and woman, beautiful frail thing, at the mercy of sickness and insanity and separation and death. In its deepest instants, it affirms both sadness and a promise. It cannot stand still; the ticking clock carefully marks the sure changes in the lovers. But the transient fulfillment, in its very sadness and pathos, points toward that which does not change, to that which makes love possible, and which vouches that love, the human love of man and woman, can at least brokenly prefigure the love that is beyond time though not excluded from time.

We are really given no choice. Now and then, whether we will it or not, we see double. We can get drunk on it and frantically try to stay drunk; we can laugh at it. Or better, we can soberly yet joyfully welcome the hints of another universe, and then examine our familiar places and days, to see whether perhaps the new universe has established colonies in our very midst.

≫ IV ≪

Invitation to Exploration

IN MY common-sense moments, I take it for granted
that I am a separate being, obviously marked off by
physical space and psychological distance from everything I perceive. Whatever I look at, I am the subject
and it is the object. I study it; I do not identify myself
with it. And steadily, I feel the unswerving flow of time.
I am growing older; the things or beings that I analyze
are changing before my eyes; I am changing. We have
our separate and lonely tempos, but time is carrying us
all in one direction.

There is also the world revealed by double vision.
The "it" I have been studying—perhaps a tree, perhaps
a man—becomes a "thou." I am no longer studying anything. Nothing is impersonal; therefore everything is
alive. The distinction between the observer and the
observed is abolished; there is simply the mutual act of
knowing and being known; "I" and "thou" are twin
suns, each revolving around the other.

When I lose myself, time loses me. "Now" is the only time; it embraces and reconciles the past, the present, the future. "Now" is time in all its fullness, and that is eternity: eternity dancing and singing through me and in me.

In the "now" that embraces all time and is not time, the splendor of all time can reveal itself, fleetingly, brokenly, but there. The gold and scarlet of all autumns is in one timeless moment of this autumn, when I see it with double vision. In a flash of love, my beloved and I are not separate from Tristan and Iseult, Abelard and Heloise, Robert and Elizabeth Browning.

But the splendor of the momentary "now" points always toward an eternal "now" which is not broken, not fleeting, not a small coral reef washed on every side by destructive time. Autumn leaves demand a gold and scarlet not at the mercy of black-gray-white winter. My beloved and I require a love that is not merely in the world, but that made the world, and is the world which endures.

These are the two worlds. The second is the one we perceive in the quick inroads of grace when time stops. Both worlds are real; both are to be taken seriously. We cannot escape the obligation of double citizenship.

How are we able to see the second world? We are

able to see it because God is the light that illumines it.
Seeing with double vision is simply seeing everything
in the light of God. Most of the time our eyes will not
respond to this light, but now and again God finds them
off guard, and then He causes them to see in His light.

It can be said another way. We see double when we
intuitively recognize that the one part of every scene
and experience that does not vary is the God Who made
all things possible. It is not essential that we recognize
God by name; we need not use any name. The moments
and flashes of double vision come to atheist and believer
alike.

But should that surprise us? God is a roving God, the
guest who comes for dinner, invited or uninvited. He
does not always knock at the door; sometimes He breaks
and enters, quietly but without shame. He stands lovingly and laughingly by the desk of the atheist who is
writing a book to prove that God does not exist. Into
the lives of men who will not or cannot call Him by
His name, He comes in disguise, taking on any name
they are capable of speaking.

Certainly it is better to know your guest by name. It
is better to invite Him for dinner before He comes any
way. It is better to have the table always set, and better
still to prepare the guest room for His permanent occu-

pation. But God has such dignity that He need not stand on appearances. Long ago He learned to sleep in a stable, and He does not hesitate to take lodgings in a corner of the attic or basement.

I suppose that if I persistently and consistently plead with God to stay away, He will at last say, "Thy will, not Mine, be done." But He is very hard to discourage; we cannot be sure whether this point of no return is ever reached in the present life. Before He gives up, He will have recourse to strong measures. If He cannot ravish you alive with beauty, He is not beyond catching you in a foxhole. He is the Father who knows no rest till the prodigal son falls at His feet and says "Father"; he cares so little for statistics that He values one sheep more than ninety-nine.

Such is the God Who is the one constant part of every double moment, and is the light by which we see double. When the moment fades and we carry our memories back to the familiar world, there is in our hearts the quiet grief of Adam and Eve trudging away from the garden, past angels armed with flaming swords. But something remains; something of deep peace and fulfillment, a wordless sense that home exists, even though we have barely glanced through the door.

We live on in hope of revisiting that home, and learning its family customs.

The foot-loose quester errs in believing he must marry a second wife when actually his first one could reveal enough of God to blind him if he really looked at her; he errs in buying a ticket to Tibet when the hill back of his home is also bathed in God's special light. The man of common sense errs in pretending that his present home, the home that the camera photographs, is his only home.

God is not someone to be pursued, nor is He someone to be disregarded. He is someone to be recognized. Once we see Him somewhere, we are better able to see Him everywhere. God wants to tease us into a voyage of exploration that will take a lifetime. Our lives have already been penetrated in quick raids. He wants us to recognize the invader.

Start with your most private moments of double seeing. Forget all I have said; think only of your own moments. What is the secret likeness that links and binds them together in your memory? You need not give it a name. But where you discern the kinship of the moments, you are seeing by the remembered light.

Start then with your moments. Then look at everything—the dishes in the sink, the letters on the desk, the tractor in the barn, a traffic sign. Are they newly revealed in the same steady light? Or at least does the memory of that light enable you to see them a little more profoundly, so that you can win some hints of the one Presence that is present in all scenes?

Let me warn you. Part Two of this book has to be, and will be, very unsystematic. It will deal with the equivalent of ships and shoes and sealing wax and cabbages and kings. If the long moments of double vision can bequeath any new understanding of ordinary days and experiences, perhaps the understanding will extend with practice to all the times and places of the commonwealth of common sense. We shall at least attempt some random samplings.

PART TWO

Exploration

⇢⇢ V ⇠⇠

A Tomato in the Autumn Sun

I COULD start anywhere. I shall start with a tomato.

A tomato plant is the poor man's apple tree. He can raise it from seed under a bit of cloth or glass, or else buy the young plants at a fraction of what he would pay for orchard trees. Any odd corner of land—as long as it has enough sunlight—will support a few tomato plants. And one growing season is sufficient for the whole cycle—seed to bud to blossom to fruit on the plant to fruit in hand.

By the time frost comes to blacken the stems and wilt the leaves, a little patch of tomato plants will have provided steady weeks of salad on the table, and enough food for meditation to last through the winter until tomato-growing weather comes again.

When I eat a tomato, it is a form of benign cannibalism. The scientists tell me—and I see no reason to doubt it—that the ancestral lines of the tomato and me cross if we trace them back far enough. At some point we were one, as unicellular creatures; then we diverged. Plants became definitely plants, animals became animals; one animal grew into the animal that is more than an animal.

Then there was a coming together again. We do not know the date. Some Indian, living in the Andes area, noticed a vine with small, bright fruit, and like a good scientist he chose to test it. He risked death by poisoning and did not die. He or his descendants subsequently went one step further: they gathered the seeds and planted them. Year by year they chose fruits that excelled in size or taste, and saved their seeds for the next year. By the time the Spanish conquistadors arrived, the tomato was being cultivated throughout the northern part of South America and in Central America.

The Indian vine now becomes a bridge across the seas. The Spaniards, zealous to introduce their way of life, destroyed much in the native civilizations; but they had no wish to destroy the tomato. It traveled to Europe early in the 16th century, and by about 1550 was delighting the Italians. Finally and much later it reached the United States from Europe, though it was long regarded as the poisonous "love apple," and the experiment of actually eating it had to be made all over again. It was not until some time in the first half of the nineteenth century that the American people in general gave their trust to this member of the nightshade family, and began raising it on a large scale.

But I am standing in my garden now, holding a tomato that I have torn in two. Without bothering to go indoors for salt, I begin nibbling at the edge of the tomato. Its ancestors and mine parted company these hundreds of millions of years ago, parted without knowing the rendezvous we should keep this crisp September day in the clear sunshine. The remote cannibalism does not disturb me. I sometimes have momentary qualms when a slice of beef on my plate suggests the horrors of the slaughter house, but a tomato is something else again. I do not think it can have a finer destiny than to delight my taste buds and feed the cells of my body.

As I turn my attention to the other half of the tomato, I notice one of the tiny, flat seeds, and put it on top of a stake, where the sun shines brightly on it. There is nothing much to see; it is very tiny. I suppose I could take it to the botany laboratory and ask one of my scientist friends to slice it into sections and put it under the microscope, so I could examine its inner structure. But this sunny day I prefer to pick another tomato and eat it, meanwhile glancing occasionally at the seed and meditating on how much miracle is capsuled within its tiny volume.

This tomato seed proclaims a God so big that He can tenderly see to little things; a God whose love is so abounding, so given to overflow, that it spills over in the form of human lives, cats, dogs, foxes, worms, trees, and tomatoes. At the moment I am particularly impressed by the love that created both me and the tomato.

Furthermore, this tomato seed proclaims the amazing freedom that God has given the human race. If I plant the seed next spring, it will normally produce a plant with fruit like that I am now eating. But I am at liberty to cross it with other strains. God Himself may throw in an occasional mutation for good measure. By patience and cunning I can develop certain types that have not existed before: new and possibly better. Certainly, the tomato I am now holding in my hand is not the wild fruit that an Indian first tested; it is not even the medium-sized tomato that the Spaniards found the Indians cultivating. I need only glance through an illustrated seed catalogue to see how mightily man has wrought since God first thrust the wild tomato into his hands.

God has made a world in which men can be His

junior partners. He does the groundwork of creation, and then permits them to share His joy by taking a wild vine and dedicating centuries to its improvement. Wars come and go, civilizations rise and topple. But there is true internationalism and progress in the centuries of coöperation that have gone into making the tomato what it is today.

God's creation of the cosmos is miracle enough; but it is no more miraculous than His special invention of one creature who can share His creativity by molding the love apple into the modern tomato.

People often speculate on whether some scientist of tomorrow will discover a way to take the raw materials of the universe and combine them into simple forms of life; then perhaps direct a process of gradual change, so that, eons later, new and complex beings will emerge from the laboratory. Thus far the prospects do not seem hopeful. But if some day man achieves this miracle, it will be merely another evidence of God's fantastic creativity, generosity, and love. It will mean that not only did He make matter from nothing, not only did He create simple life and guide it to greater development and responsibility, but He actually produced one form of life—man—so completely built in His own image that it can backtrack to the time of nonliving matter and from there repeat the mighty acts of God.

But the sun is pleasantly warm, despite a certain crispness in the air. I know that soon the first frosts will come to blacken my tomato plants, and wilt the wild purple asters growing at the edge of the garden. The sadness that accompanies all endings is salt to the other half of my second tomato. How transient the life of a tomato plant is, and on how many gifts in combination it is dependent: soil, water, sun, warmth, an atmosphere free of poisons—and my own willingness to plant and hoe and fertilize.

It seems presumptuous to hope that next year all these gifts will exist in the right combination. When frost makes its first onslaught, the idea of another spring will be a sheer act of faith, resting in confidence that God is both loving and reliable.

Again I look at the seed. Locked inside of it is perhaps a billion years of living history, and a plant that wants to climb toward the sun. I doubt that God will disappoint it.

➤➤➤ VI ⧏⧏⧏

Desolation and Extravagance

THE GLOBE on which we live is not a tomato; we cannot slice off little bits and eat them. There are parts of the earth where we survive only by taking our food and oxygen along, or wearing clothing as bizarre as anything in science fiction.

It is easy to see God's light reflected from a ripe tomato; at such times the earth becomes our private garden. But what of the explorers who travel to the Antarctic and cross ice whose oldest layers are estimated to be two million years old?

One need not cross Antarctica to discover that much of the earth is not a vegetable garden. The Englishman, journeying to the Scottish highlands, and finding a world better adapted to nourish the black-faced sheep than their owners, learns this truth soon enough. The Bedouin Arab knows it almost from birth.

In America, a New Englander or a Virginian, accustomed to soft green hills, will quickly learn the same lesson if he drives through parts of New Mexico and Arizona. It is as though a spaceship had marooned him on the moon; his memories afterward are a confused blur of desolation. The crumbling chains of mountains look like slag heaps dumped by unfriendly giants. The evergreens, scattered at wide intervals, suggest the clumps of coarse grass that take root on refuse heaps outside a city.

The desert itself is sometimes without apparent life—nothing but sand blown by the wind into shifting ripples. At other places, when it is closely examined it is frighteningly full of life—the kind one sees in nightmares: scorpions, and poisonous snakes. And outlined against the horizon, like a surrealist painting, are the cactus plants, beautiful in their flowering season, but wearing always the savage spines that are their *noli me tangere*. Then there are the dark red mesas off in the distance, like the truncated ruins of pyramids left by a rumored race. The total impression is of a world not built for man.

As you drive along a concrete highway it is very difficult to believe that in twenty-five or fifty miles there will be a filling station, a motel, a drug store, fresh drinking water.

You are tempted to ask yourself whether even God

belongs in this world. Has some dark power, some anti-god, been at work here, carving out his private domain?

No. There is no anti-god if by that we mean a rival god; there is only one God. And the desert is God's, though it is not man's.

The difficulty is that we expect the world to be our tomato. The tomato is part of the world that God has brought into being, but His plans are wider and stranger than men and tomatoes.

I can give you an analogy. When I go in to see the president of my college, he listens and talks as though he had unlimited leisure. He gives his attention and himself utterly to my words; he never glances at his watch. Yet I know that his appointment calendar is always full. When I rise and he tells me good-bye, someone is waiting in his reception room. It may be a member of the Board of Trustees, prepared to discuss financial or administrative matters that I could only dimly comprehend, though on them perhaps depends the welfare of the college and my own. I recognize that I am only part of the college, and that the president concerns himself with all of it, even those portions that might only bewilder me if he explained them to me.

Of course, the president cannot talk with me about my hopes and problems and simultaneously discuss an endowment drive with a trustee; he has to take us one at a time. But God can take us all at a time and still be listening and talking to each of us individually. He can and does preside over the garden patch and the desert with equal solicitude.

The desert proclaims God, because it is there, and for the most part man is not. Each cactus plant, each mesa, each slapheap of a mountain is a public notice, reading, "This is Mine. I made it. I was God before there were any valleys, any deserts, any planets, any stars. I was God while My earth rotated its lifeless face to the sun. I was God when only one-celled creatures invisibly lived on My earth. I was God when the great reptiles rooted in the swamps and flapped their clumsy wings through the fetid air. I am God. I shall be God, though you poison the air with cobalt and destroy every living thing on this globe. I was, I am, I am to be. I am that I am."

It is no accident that solitary men, drifting in a boat far out at sea and seemingly alone in its immensity, have been ravished by the certainty of God's presence. It is no accident that the first sure knowledge of God was given to a race of desert wanderers, caught between a blazing sun and fiery sand.

God would be a diminished God if we had to believe

that His whole creation were our garden patch. He is so vast a God that His master plan includes paragraphs for snakes and scorpions and cactus plants, as well as cows, horses, tomatoes, and men.

What is the master plan, as it pertains to snakes and cactus plants? We cannot possibly know. What knowledge does a rattlesnake have of Jesus Christ and His atoning death? How can we divine what revelation and destiny is written by God in the rattlesnake's heart? To us is revealed what we need to know; the rest is in God's mind and His secret hands.

Certainly, the God proclaimed alike by tomato plant and cactus plant is not given to narrow husbandry and petty prudence. He creates the stars and island universes with extravagant abandon. Though there may be millions upon millions of planets, it seems almost certain that relatively few of them have the right temperature and atmosphere to support life of our kind. Despite science fiction, the prospects for Mars and Venus are not good. Perhaps the earth and its inhabitants are rare cosmic exceptions. But should this disturb us?

If most of God's universe is inhospitable, this does not mean that He is a poor host; He merely created parts of it for purposes other than ours. It is all written down in the master plan, though these particular paragraphs have not been revealed to us.

Conjecture will do no harm. Perhaps God creates stars and planets with abandon simply because He likes to create them. It may be that the esthetic sense which all men have in some degree can trace its source to the Supreme Esthete, Who is not ashamed at times to practice art for art's sake.

Meanwhile and in any event as I write these words the creatures of the desert go about obeying the imperatives of their nature, and the stars and planets conform to the laws of the loving Mind that made them.

⇶ VII ⇜

Metropolis

THE TOMATO and the desert and the extravagant reaches of space all proclaim God; but they do not clearly reveal His sociability.

God has never been lonely. If, as some scientists think, the universe came into existence at a definite "time," God was still not lonely, even though He was alone before He created the universe. The reason that God cannot be lonely is that within His very being there is the giving and receiving of love. This is true because there is a threeness within the oneness of the one God. From all eternity the Father loves the Son and the Holy Spirit; the Son loves the Father and the Holy Spirit; the Holy Spirit loves the Father and the Son. It has been a three-cornered exchange of gifts from all time and before all time; a loving competition in courtesy and hospitality. No wonder love reached such an intensity that it overflowed and created galaxies, dinosaurs, and men.

The City of God, which hovers and infiltrates and tantalizes, but whose complete visibility must wait until all things are Christ's, as Christ is already God's—the City of God is this divine courtesy, sociability, and love, with the doors open for everyone to come in. When the invitation has been accepted by all who will, and the chairs at the banquet table are all taken, the City will fully exist.

Now in the interim period, when the vision exists but fades and shines and fades again, the city of man must exist also, to point toward the other City, as a piece of sheet music points toward the universes that a composer has found and explored; universes that exist, though we might not know it, except for one explorer.

Take New York, Paris, London, San Francisco—imperial, queenly cities. Common sense accurately sees everything that is wrong with them, which is almost everything. Some have gangsters, some have smog, all have slums, all have thieves, in all of them is the brutal Darwinian struggle.

But these things are no more the city than a cancer is the man. Imperfection is the broken reflection of perfection; evil is good turned sour. In the city, the very thieves who practice, for evil ends, their own kind of loyalty are abusing, but also using, a virtue that God implants in bankers and bank robbers alike. Evil can exist only because good comes first.

The deepest purpose of the earthly city is to be a working model of The City—a clumsy and imperfect one, but sufficiently accurate, when viewed through the eyes of double seeing, to point toward that which it temporarily prefigures.

The earthly city cannot escape goodness. It draws men from hundreds and thousands of miles to teach them the secret of working together in an unlimited interrelatedness. Trucks, trains, planes, and ships pour materials into it, to be processed and exported. What comes as raw grain goes back as boxed cereals; metal ore is turned into jewelry, Diesel engines, flutes, scientific instruments. Money is converted into shares, and shares into businesses that provide goods for the world and living for workers.

The magnet of the city is especially powerful for men with specialized talents. In the city are congregated the philosophers, in a symbiotic relation with other philosophers, magazines, and publishing houses; here writers meet writers and artists meet artists and scientists meet scientists. More often than one might imagine, saints meet saints. Excellence is brought to a finer and more useful edge by contact with other excellence.

To see the city as it is, to see it reflecting and pre-figuring the glory of the eternal City, you need only look at a traffic signal, or listen to the policeman's whistle. Here is the meeting-point between freedom and order, the deliberate creation and acceptance of authority in order that freedom may grow rather than decline. A traffic jam represents the virtual absence of freedom. A steadily moving stream of traffic, halting only at the command of the reasonable red light or the policeman's whistle, is the freedom that comes from the creation and acceptance of order.

But this is still the earthly city, not the City of God. Necessary authority and order on earth are always imperfectly exercised and grudgingly accepted. In the City of God the words "freedom" and "order" are obsolescent; their meanings coalesce into the meaning of love. In the City of God love creates—spontaneously creates—its own ecstatic order, and freedom consists of the freedom to love.

➤➤➤ VIII ⫷⫷⫷

The Politician as Physician

THIS is as good a place as any to look again at the voyage of exploration in which we are engaged, and to be quite clear about its purpose.

We began with the private moments of double sight, when a door briefly opens. In all those moments we sensed the presence of God, as the unvarying part of the moment; and what we fleetingly saw we saw in His light.

The present voyage is to various landscapes, human and not. In looking at them, in thinking about them, we do not expect any door to open at our command—the moments of opening are deeds of grace, and these cannot be commanded. But it seems reasonable to assume that if at all times we remember the moments of special vision, we shall detect something akin to them—though less vivid and compelling by one degree—in every scene and experience. In a word, we are hoping to find, if not God, at least His footprints.

We know that God is a rover. The Father is ever carrying on the work of creation, large-scale and small; and He is also in constant search of lost sheep and prodigal sons. His only-begotten Son is filled with the same restless love; it gives Him no peace until all creatures are in His peace. The Holy Spirit eddies like the untrammeled wind to make all things holy.

Therefore the particular places we visit during the voyage of exploration do not greatly matter; if we find God's footprints in one, we can expect to find them in all.

Our recent visit to the city of man revealed the many ways in which it haltingly prefigures the City of God. From the metropolis we travel easily to politics, the art by which the functioning of the earthly city is made possible. If we remember what we saw in the quick eternities of double sight, may we not detect something kindred in the work of the politician?

We can. A good politician is like a good physician. The physician is a trained and dedicated man, who fights a running battle against disease, accident, and death. He does not create the human body, nor is he the inventor of that amazing well of life within it, but he coöperates with what is already there. Most of the time he does relatively simple things. He clears up an infection with miracle drugs; he removes a corrupt appendix. But at times he is compelled to be daring: he removes a kidney or a lung for the sake of the total body; he transplants pieces of bone or artery; he probes the recesses of the brain itself. Often he must work with death in his hands, for death is still more certain if he does not work.

The politician is the physician of the social body. He does not create the life and fundamental health that already exist; that is given by God, implanted, a reflection of the sociability of the Trinity. So great is this heritage that much of history simply records how the social nature of the human race has gradually broadened to take in larger and larger groups. The agony through which the world is now passing is comparable to that of the late Middle Ages and Renaissance, when the petty dukedoms of western Europe were being cemented, by blood and fire, into nations. Today the whole world is agonized at not being one.

The work of the politician exists in all magnitudes from the village to the United Nations; but everywhere it is the same work. The good politician begins by giving thanks for the deep health that already exists, no matter how many diseases may constantly threaten it. Without this God-given health, nothing could be done. The politician can no more create civic health *ex nihilo* that he can snap his fingers and tell a new solar system to leap into existence.

He cannot create it; but he can coöperate with it. This he does by trying to understand the true goal of society, and by working with those forces that lead toward the goal.

The ultimate goal is love. It must be made to prevail as far and as deep as men will consent. But love cannot be legislated, though legislation can remove obstacles to its free flow. For the most part, the legislator must aim at justice, which is love at a distance of fifty paces. Justice need not be a cold and static word. A gradual process of infiltration has occurred, so that "justice" has taken on some of the overtones of "love." It no longer means, "Leave me alone and I'll leave you alone," or "It is equally illegal for poor men and rich men to sleep in the public parks." Thanks to the prophets whom God sends into all His political parties, justice is becoming positive as well as negative. Justice has come to mean free schools, social security, protection for oppressed groups; in general, an outgoing concern for everyone, rather than the mere building of barbed wire entanglements to keep out trespassers. All this is still not the Kingdom of God in its fullness, but it offers clear, shining hints of what that Kingdom will reveal.

The politician is like the physician in his perceptive coöperation with the health that already exists. But there is a further resemblance. A physician repelled by a body not in perfect health would be both a logical contradiction and a dubious friend of the sick; he must learn to work in the sick room. In the same way, the good politician needs to be equally at home in the book-lined study and the smoke-filled room.

In the smoke-filled room the politician quickly becomes aware of the stubborn limitations that exist in a given society at a given moment. He learns the prejudices, rational or irrational, of classes and groups. He senses the fears—all the more powerful for being only half-formulated. He learns the hopes, legitimate and illegitimate, of the "interests." He must balance Wisconsin butter against Southern cottonseed oil, and both against the housewife's budget. He must weigh simultaneously the concerns of domestic industry, the Swiss watchmakers, and all the ramifications of world trade.

The physician who is too great an extremist has

licensed himself as the angel of death. He may remove one diseased lung or kidney; he dare not remove both. The politician, like the physician, is aiming at maximum health, and must judge each situation as he meets it: which course of action will be best calculated to cure whatever diseases are curable, while he avoids the likelihood of excessive shock.

In the quiet study, the good politician sees a hovering ideal: it is the City of God. In the smoke-filled room he learns how far the city of man is from that ideal. He must begin with the earthly city as it is. He does not despair: he has seen the vision; he knows the right direction of travel; he can afford to be patient.

I have been praising the politician who is not ashamed to compromise on half a loaf. But the city of man also needs the person who serves by being an unpopular pathfinder, decades or centuries ahead of his time. The early abolitionists, subject to mayhem in North and South alike, prepared the way for the practical Lincoln, who moved easily back and forth between the quiet study and the smoke-filled room. A doctrinnaire and rigid Wilson was the forerunner of the pragmatic Roosevelt and the United Nations. Churchill, in mid-course proclaiming the unpleasant truth that some infamies cannot be appeased, awoke England into readiness for its ordeal of greatest splendor, and prepared his own path and that of his nation for the postwar rebuilding of a broken world. Thoreau, living in his hut at Walden Pond in a state of virtual secession from society, was actually camped in one of the public parks of the city of man, for his lonely ideas have since become the property of mankind; Gandhi, for instance, was in large part indebted to Thoreau for the concept of civil disobedience.

One scarcely needs to point out how visibly God is at work in the abolitionists or in a Thoreau. It is equally essential to recognize the witness of the endlessly patient men who deal day by day with the hopes, the sicknesses, the fluctuating life of society, and who make themselves at home in the smoke-filled room because it is one of mankind's homes. To adopt an attitude of proud superiority toward them is tantamount to disparaging God because He deigned to be born in a stable.

It is futile to talk about politics and politicians until you have had some experience, however marginal, in politics. I shall speak for myself. It has been my good fortune to know and even for a short time to work with one of the really towering political figures of our times. I was able to observe his complete dedication, the solicitude of the dedicated physician. I have seen how he is guided by the hovering vision, though he can talk the technicalities of politics with any precinct captain. I have sensed the agony that is his when the vision collides head-on with the intractable limitations of any society at a particular moment in its history. But I have not seen him turn to bitterness or despair or cynicism. The vision remains; he works toward it as far and as fast as he can.

This experience has made me look again at politics in general. I think I can now see it with flashes of double sight. As I observe the mayors, governors, assemblymen, Congressmen, Cabinet members and other politicians about me, I do not admire all of them. Some seem seriously mistaken in their ideas; some are stupid; a few have the evil of demons in their hearts. All this is merely to say that they are human beings, and vary as other mortals do. But in the majority of politicians I now discern, to a varying degree, an awareness of the hovering ideal, and some recognition of the city of man as a groping toward the City of God.

All social contrivances are clumsy and imperfect, and those who devise them are mere men. But thanks be to the patient men who are willing to be clumsy and imperfect in order that the eternal harmony and sociability of the blessed Trinity may be less brokenly reflected and prefigured in the city of man. And praised be God, Who sent His Son into a stable, and sends His prophets into smoke-filled rooms.

⇒⇒ IX ⇐⇐

Where Need Is, There Christ Is Also

GOD can be seen at work in politics—some politics. But to recognize Him there is one of the severest tests of double sight. The larger the number of people in any relationship, the more mixed is the good that is possible. In the intricate and impersonal operations of society, the highest practical good is often justice tinged with love, and this blend does not shine as brightly as simple love—love that engulfs justice and makes the separate word unnecessary.

When one man meets another, love exists more easily than when millions intermesh with millions, and God is easier to recognize.

This is an obvious truth, but it recently came home to me with double power when I reread a short story that has long haunted me, *Where Love Is, There God Is Also*. This tale, one of the simplest that Tolstoy ever wrote, has an old shoemaker as its central character. He lives and works in a basement room with one window, through which he can watch the passing shoes and boots of the city people.

The shoemaker is a religious man, and spends a great deal of his spare time reading the New Testament. One night he turns to Luke, and is absorbed in the story of the rich Pharisee who invited Christ to dinner, and the sinful woman who washed His feet with her tears and then anointed them. The old fellow begins to wonder whether he is as blind as the irritated Pharisee. Would he fail to notice the presence in his midst if Christ were to visit him some day?

He falls asleep. Suddenly he hears a voice calling him by name. Sleepily glancing around, he sees no one. He dozes off again. Then once more he hears the voice, and it adds, "Look tomorrow on the street. I am coming." The shoemaker rises from his chair, sees no one, and goes to bed.

The next day he is back at his usual work, but he cannot forget the mysterious voice, though he is uncertain whether it was merely a dream.

This particular day, whenever anyone passes by the window, he bends down low so he can see the face as well as the boots.

Soon he notices an old soldier outside, laboriously shoveling the snow off the sidewalk. A strange fancy seizes the shoemaker. Suppose this were Christ? He laughs at himself for the absurdity, and goes back to his work. But he is restless. He looks out the window again, and sees how weary the old soldier has become after a few minutes of shoveling. On an impulse he invites him in, and gives him tea. They talk of Christ and His love for the poor and sinful.

The broken-down soldier leaves. The shoemaker works some more, but continually pauses to peer out the window. Soon he sees a woman, dressed in thin summer clothes, trying to pacify a crying baby. He asks them in, and plays with the baby while its mother eats bread and cabbage soup. When she leaves, he gives her a coat and enough money to reedem her shawl from the pawnbroker.

After another interlude of work, the shoemaker looks out the window again, and sees an old apple-woman wearily resting. While he watches, a little boy dashes up, and snatches one of her apples. She seizes him by his sleeve and holds him squirming.

The shoemaker runs outside and with some difficulty persuades the apple-woman not to drag the boy off to the police station for a whipping. Finally, the little boy, now contrite, offers to carry the woman's bag, and the two walk off together, almost as mother and son.

Back once more in his basement room, the old shoe-maker works a while longer, and then notices that it is getting dark. He lights his lamp. Soon he takes his Testament down from the shelf. He intends to begin where he was reading the day before, but by chance the book opens at another place.

Suddenly he remembers his dream. Simultaneously he hears steps behind him. He looks around, and half discerns people standing in the dark corner.

"It was I," a voice says, and the old soldier steps forth and quickly vanishes. "And it was I," says the same voice, and the woman with her baby steps forth, the woman smiling and the child laughing; they quickly vanish. "And it was I," the voice continues as the apple-woman and the boy come out, and then quickly vanish.

Filled with joy, the shoemaker crosses himself, and begins to read the Gospels where the book has chanced to open. He reads: *For I was an hungred, and ye gave me meat: I was thirsty, and ye gave me drink: I was a stranger, and ye took me in.* Then his eye travels down to the bottom of the page: *Inasmuch as ye have done it unto one of the least of these my brethren, ye have done it unto me.*

Then the shoemaker knows Who has visited him three times that day and Whom he has received.

Christ revealed that all need is His need. Any hungry baby is a hungry Christ child; any weary traveler is the traveler who walked many weary miles to preach and minister; any man in pain anywhere is the nailed Christ. Christ, by knowing need, has raised it from the animal or merely human. Whoever suffers need, has the suffering Christ within him. Whoever gives food or drink or meets any other human need is serving the needy Christ. Whoever serves Christ is serving God, with Whom Christ is one.

To find Christ you do not need to leave your block; you do not need to leave your house. Where the needs of food and drink and clothing and medicine do not exist, there are other needs as imperious: a child wishing to learn the alphabet, a wife with more dishes than she can conveniently do, a friend whose need is simply but desperately for someone with patience, sympathy, and listening ears.

Yet it is true that Christ most frequently commands the simplest acts of helpfulness: food, drink, clothing, shelter, medical care; these have priority. Therefore the face of Christ is likely to be most clearly visible when one is ministering to the bluntest needs. Of the men of our day, I think Albert Schweitzer has seen that face as often as any; he is Christ-surrounded. The face of Christ appears to him with the full lips and dark skin of the African natives, and it is a face of sickness and suffering; such a face as would not permit the great theologian, philosopher, and musician to remain in comfortable Europe.

This is a knowledge of Christ that transcends all theory. I can read Schweitzer's brilliant early book, *The Quest of the Historical Jesus,* alternately admiring its insights and deploring what I still believe to be its distortions and blind spots. I can finish the book with gratitude for the many ways it has deepened my comprehension of Christ, yet still convinced that the Nicene Creed is more accurate.

At this point the great temptation enters—and how plausibly! I am tempted to take a man's words and equate them with the complete man. If I do that, I may have the appalling presumption to say, "In such and such ways, this man is heretical."

But if I speak these words, who has the right to stay the lightning of God's judgment? Who am I, living the comfortable life of a college professor in civilized Wisconsin, to judge the orthodoxy of Albert Schweitzer?

If his theoretical formulations of Christian belief depart from what I consider the truth—if he is plain mistaken at points, as I believe he is—I still have not earned the right to speak loudly. Does not my comfortable way of life depart still more from the ultimate orthodoxy? In what way am I ministering directly and constantly to the needs of the latent Christ? Through my teaching and preaching and writing, I hope—but this is hope, not certainty. There is no ambiguity about the Christ Whom Dr. Schweitzer beholds many times a day.

When we respond to God's prior love by an outgoing love to meet human needs, that is the final orthodoxy. At the eventual meeting of Schweitzer and the visible, glorified Christ, there will be no need for any letter of introduction; it will be the reunion of old friends. Some of us at best will fumble over our words at the climactic moment, and the face will not be precisely the countenance we have pictured in our fancy.

It is not, of course, that all of us are called to find Christ as Schweitzer finds Him. Some are called to be soil conservationists or lawyers or teachers or policemen or soldiers or labor union leaders or business men or housewives and mothers. Some are called to poverty, chastity, and obedience, and the life of constant prayer. Some are called to paint pictures that not five of their friends will like, or to write poems that not a roomful of people in a large town will comprehend. All these activities meet the needs, the infinitely varied and divine needs, of the hidden Christ.

But if there must be a hierarchy, I believe the Schweitzers will be found (to their own astonishment) standing near the front, with the great martyrs and confessors and apostles, when the only really valid order of precedence is some day made manifest.

❯❯❯ X ❮❮❮

The Bowing Order

But is there a hierarchy among the redeemed in heaven? Of this much I think we can be sure: no one will bow to anyone else, or everyone will bow to everyone else. I believe it will be the latter.

But, it may be asked, is not God enough? Will not the redeemed prefer to spend their eternity kneeling in grateful adoration before God and standing to praise His holy Name?

It is true that if you have God, you have everything. But then—and only then—do you begin to understand everything. What you have given to God, He blesses and returns. Consider the mystic who renounces blue skies and green trees in order to enter the darkness where God is a deeper darkness. He finds God—Who thereupon sends him back to see how blue is blue and how green is green, and to give thanks to the Lord Artisan who invented the spectrum. The fasting of Lent terminates in the feasting of Easter.

God is not so brutal a radiance that He makes it impossible for our wounded eyes to see other beings. He is the light in which we see all beings as they are.

We shall all kneel to God in heaven, and stand to praise Him: granted, and obviously. But if we are to mirror the sociability and gaiety and courtesy of the Trinity, there will also be leisure to bow to one another in a pattern so intricate and laughing that it will be more a square dance than a receiving line.

Few of us can bow without feeling foolish. That is because our ancestors made the discovery that louts and clods often inherited a social position they could never have earned. The gap between personal merit and official status called forth the purgation of satires, barbed songs, and revolutionary movements. Sincerity triumphed with the equalitarian handshake, which greets a man simply because he is a man. And the fraternal hand—say of a French taxi driver at the end of the trip—has its own splendor and rightness.

But it is one thing to bow to a man because his great-grandfather merited a bow; it is quite a different thing to bow to him because *he* deserves it—though he may have been born in the slums, though his English may be awkward, though his face may be the kind you would not notice when you first come into a room.

The real hierarchy, which is obscured but not abolished by the equalitarian handshake, is not arranged in the neat layers of the sociological classifications. Neither in heaven nor on earth is a man completely "middle upper" or "upper middle" or "middle lower." He can be in all nine strata, for there are more than nine sides to a man.

Should Schweitzer and Shakespeare meet in heaven, Schweitzer will bow to the poet, and Shakespeare to the saint. Perhaps Shakespeare's bow will be deeper, but both will bow. And it may be that the exquisite courtesy in which saints are schooled will dictate that the reverse be true. (Shakespeare, of course, will bow also to the organist, the student of Bach, the theologian, the philosopher.)

We are starved for hierarchy. A young man joining a service club is compelled against his deep needs to call graybeards by their first names; everywhere is the pressure toward flat uniformity. But the need remains: we want to revere that which deserves reverence.

Here and there our hunger is partly satisfied. We dare show special respect to a president or king, because presidency and kingship are inherently worthy of respect, no matter who the president or king may be. But these are merely small islands of hierarchy; in daily life we live increasingly on the flat plain of the equalitarian handshake.

Perhaps it must be so. In this interim period of life on the earth, as life is, there is no one-for-one correspondence between the man and the symbol. If we relearned the habit of bowing, there would be confusion. Should we be showing reverence for the man himself, or for that which he symbolizes? The handshake avoids confusion, but at the cost of spiritual undernourishment.

Christian legend has always arranged the angels in ranks; the devil is said to have his own "lowerarchy." The human hierarchy we intuitively seek is that of the Christ-servers. The old shoemaker found Christ in a broken-down soldier, in a drab woman and her baby, in the apple-woman and a street urchin. But such is the courtesy of Christ that He fills us with desire to honor those who serve Him. May I not bow to the shoemaker?

In heaven the confusion between symbol and man will be removed, along with all other confusions. There will be no man with a title he does not deserve; every man who deserves a title will have it. I can bow to the woman who made superlative blackberry pies to the glory of God and the delight of man. She can curtsy to me—for something, I hope. I do not think there will be

[79]

found in heaven anyone so devoid of talents in Christ's service that he will never receive a bow or curtsy. The square dance will mount in gaiety. Laughter and bows and curtsies will be woven into a pattern that changes and flashes and responds always with the exquisite accuracy of love to the music and the Caller.

⇛ XI ⇚

The Church and the Church Outside the Church

BUT THE square dance of heaven in all its splendor and gaiety lies ahead, partly hidden by the thin curtain that loosely hangs between faith and knowledge. We are given sufficient hints now so that nothing in the dance will surprise us utterly—though nothing will be precisely as we expected.

For the time being, if we want a foretaste of heaven we shall do well to redefine the quest and ask simply, "Where am I most certain of finding Christ?" Or, better yet, "Where am I most likely to recognize that He has already found me?"

The logical place to begin your search is the Church. And you will not be disappointed. The Church, in its time-transcending, space-transcending, denomination-transcending reality, is Christ's body, maintaining a visible continuity with that human body that once walked the roads of Palestine.

Go then to a local church, one cell in the universal Church, and a miniature of it. When the congregation assembles, Christ assembles with them. He promised that He would.

Go, if possible, to the Holy Communion, when Christ out of love makes Himself as common as food and drink. Words of remembrance and blessing are spoken at the altar, words that flow backward toward the Thursday evening when Jesus met in an upper room for a farewell supper with His disciples. The words flow backward and engulf that Thursday; they swerve swiftly to encircle a manger; they race forward and carry with them the best of all Fridays and the Sunday that has made of every Sunday a small Easter. The birth of Christ, His atoning death, His Resurrection—these are no longer remote memories, embedded and embalmed in a sacred book. Time is abolished. We are beside Christ in Bethlehem and Jerusalem. He is beside us, here and now.

As we kneel at the altar rail for the bread and wine that are now Christ's body and blood, we are no longer separate from one another—no longer separate from Christ. All bodies are one body, all blood is one common store of blood. And the one Crucifixion and the one

Resurrection are reënacted within us, so that we too may die and live again. Yet it is not we that live, but the Christ Who has lovingly invaded us in this time-devouring moment.

The moment fades easily—as moments do; other thoughts and future worries crowd in. Sometimes—many times—there is no vivid consciousness of Christ's presence, even at the moment of receiving His body and blood. This is not because Christ is absent, but because we are. Our thoughts are distracted by a discordant choir, memories of a fumbling sermon, private antagonisms, plans for practical deeds next day.

But whether we recognize the Guest or not, He faithfully comes. We do not merit His visits; even in our most attentive and faithful moments we do not merit them. If we had to be worthy of the Guest, we should never have the privilege of receiving Him. But we are not asked to be worthy; rather, we are asked to know that we are not worthy, and to say so. He will come. Whenever two or three are gathered together in the Name of Christ, He is there. He promised.

He is there, in the Church. He is there no matter how feebly those who meet in His name are able to mirror the life that moves in their midst. But He is not in the Church only.

[83]

If by "the Church" we mean the visible Church of those who call themselves Christians, how can we say that Christ is there and there only? Can we tie the feet of the eternal Second Person of the Trinity? Those restless feet were ever at the service of any human need. The Christ of the Gospels walked many painful miles to preach and minister. Do we believe that He has grown lazy and indifferent? He goes and will always go where He is needed. His love is as restless and unrelenting as human hate.

We may say, if we wish, that Christ is never found outside the Church, but we must add in the same breath that wherever Christ is, there is the Church. Christ is both the Head of the Church and its best definition. Therefore if He chooses at certain times and places to work through a faculty meeting, a collective bargaining session, or a convention of the National Association of Manufacturers, there, for the moment at least, is the Church.

The total Church—that Church whose being is defined by Christ's presence—is too big to be contained within the visible Church. It breaks the walls; it overflows; it invades and transforms the strangest places and moments.

This second Church, the unofficial one, exists with

many purposes. One of them is to do the things that the visible Church should have done. Race relations will serve as a convenient example. The visible Church should have provided the leadership and spirit for a gradual, persistent and loving elimination of the artificial barriers that separate fellow men—even fellow Christians—because of race. But wherever these barriers have been toppled or eroded away, it has been as often as not the work of men and women not conspicuously identified with the Church. Too frequently the visible Church has given the impression of waiting for others with courage enough to do the necessary job, and then eagerly rushing on the stage to claim all the credit possible.

Race relations are only one instance of many. The work of infusing "justice" with the overtones of love, of making it positive as well as negative, owes as much to secular humanitarians as to Church leaders. One could spell this out in detail, but the fact hardly needs elaborate documentation.

Those who do Christ's work in His spirit if not explicitly in His name are on His side, whether they know it or not, and we who watch them from within the visible Church can only confess our own slowness and timidity, and offer praises to a God Who is big enough to find the visible Church too small for His total plan.

Sometimes sacred walls must be thrown down, not so much to let the world in as to let the Church out. When I first saw the ruins of Glastonbury Abbey—the lovely and poignant fragments of a church that was larger than most of the English cathedrals—my first thought was, "Could any reform be worth this price?" A heavy price it was indeed—the dissolution of the monasteries under Henry VIII; it left the British landscape haunted with ruins. But then I thought of the British people today—of their quiet kindliness, their determination to create a nation from which brutality and want are banished as far as humanly possible. I began to see that possibly—in God's eyes—these ruins did not represent wanton sacrilege. I do not presume to read His thoughts, but it may be that Christianity was too much bottled up within walls—bottled up and in danger of stagnating. Perhaps many walls had to come down, so that what they had cherished could penetrate more profoundly into ordinary homes and secular streets.

I am not sure. But these were the thoughts that came slowly to me as I stood in the midst of the haunting and heartbreaking devastation of passions and centuries.

Such a train of thought can be carried very far. Some

have asserted that the only goal of Christianity is humanitarianism, and that the visible Church will gradually and properly be superseded by the unofficial one—perhaps in the form of organized benevolence and the welfare state. Let us look at this. Is it true that Christ is more easily recognized—and increasingly more active—in the various branches of the unofficial Church than in the visible one?

This is escaping from one distortion by running to its opposite. The assertion implies that Christ is in limited supply; but He is not. He may pull down some walls, but not all. He is fully present in both His Churches. He uses them to maintain a dialogue of mutual correction and stimulation. The unofficial Church constantly shames its visible brother into remembering that it ought to be what it is—the body of Christ: His lips, His hands, His feet. But the visible Church has a service it can render to the unofficial Church: it can remind the secular idealist of the roots of his idealism. Almost always he has either learned his concern for his fellows in church (and then left church, because it has not practiced what it taught him), or he has gained it as his heritage of centuries shaped by the Christian Gospel, or finally his concern has been planted in his mind and heart—directly—by the same imperious and loving God Who is the Father of Jesus Christ.

If I believed that God could work only through the visible Church, He would be a hobbled and diminished God. But He can raise up apostles from the very stones; He can and does recruit His soldiers and workers from the ranks of many who refuse to speak the Name that they honor by serving. We in the visible Church can teach them a correct vocabulary. But let us keep silence long enough to find what they can teach us, for their deeds give evidence that they have been secretly instructed by the One Who faithfully meets with us whenever two or three are gathered together in His Name.

⟫⟫ XII ⟪⟪

Work

THIS VOYAGE of exploration is necessarily my voyage first, and yours second. I have been exploring the sights and experiences that particularly interest me: tomatoes, politics, and many others.

My interests may not be yours. Perhaps you can better discern God's footsteps elsewhere: in the mechanism of the human eye, the history of the steam engine, or the structure of international trade. A football game or the numinous mysteries of laughter may be your best area of exploration. Then close the book a while and meditate on your private clues to God's presence. I think you will find His footprints, and gleams of His light. When you are ready, open the book again, and go direct to Part Three.

Possibly, though, you may wish to carry on with me a while longer. In that event, the next search for rumors of the light will concern an activity shared by man and God: work. It is not a wholly pleasant subject.

Work, as we usually know it, is evidence that Paradise has really been lost; it is a curse visited on the mutinous Adam and his descendants. It teaches the same stern lesson as the flaming swords turning in every direction to bar the road back.

God, however, is a redeemer, because He is also a lover. With His help, can work be redeemed? Can it become a joy?

Even though Paradise has been lost, certain kinds of work retain its traces. We still bear God's image within us—pitifully scarred and marred, but not defaced past recognition. Something of God's outgoing restlessness, His delight in making things that have not existed before, is given us with His image. The joy is seen at its clearest when the work is the most playful. A child building castles of sand for the high tide to sweep away is God-like in his pure creativity.

Still, God is not merely playful; His playthings are often useful. Surely this is true of that portion of creation that we know best. It is crammed with such useful things as atmosphere, topsoil, water, and minerals. It is the kind of world in which all sorts of creatures can live and multiply. Indeed, God seems to practice at times an ingenuous economy. He invents a thing as lovely as the human mouth, and adapts it to multiple purposes: eating, kissing, speech.

Useful playfulness is found in some trades. The shoemaker in Tolstoy's story was privileged to be God-like. He could carry through the process of shoemaking from leather to finished article. Every time he looked out the basement window there was a good chance of seeing his sturdy work go past, protecting the feet of his fellow men from the cold Russian winter.

A more familiar example of useful playfulness is a housewife planning and cooking every part of an elaborate meal, or sewing her daughter's first party dress. An inner vision becomes tangible in that which is created; there is the conviction, "I saw this through from idea to object."

The curse of Adam rests rather lightly on the shoemaker and the housewife; they may know sweat on the brow, but at least their work has built-in significance. Yet they are sinful mortals, and must reckon with some share of Adam's legacy. The need for money and the whims of public taste can compel the shoemaker to produce footware of a design that offends his esthetic sense or is poorly adapted to the human foot. The housewife perhaps finds herself preparing a beautiful dinner for people she loathes, or making the party dress in response to constant nagging on the part of an impatient daughter. Whenever some kind of external necessity exists, one better understands the stern words of the Lord to the banished Adam.

At any rate, the housewife and the shoemaker are fortunate compared to the opposite extreme—say, an assembly-line worker. He is the one really prepared to search and interpret the Scriptures. He finds himself eight hours a day at a task that seldom changes—perhaps he screws the left fender onto one chassis after another, as each remains a carefully timed moment in front of him. He may never have visited the foundry where the castings are made for the engine; he will never know who buys the finished car; he would have no way of recognizing it if he saw it on the street. Then what is his joy? the weekly check?

I have often wondered what someone who thoroughly enjoys his own work could say to the assembly-line worker. The latter often reaches his maximum of skill in a few months. He finds himself doing, time after time, fractions of work that a machine could almost do. Frequently he has come from very far away, and his human ties to loved places and faces have been snapped. He lives in a sprawling and depersonalized city. I fear that anything one can say will sound remote and abstract.

The difficulty is compounded by one important circumstance: this is not a period of history in which the imagination flourishes. The schools and other shapers of public mentality do their efficient best to stamp it out, in favor of application to practical problems and processes. But I do not see any way toward profound fulfillment for the assembly line worker at his task, unless he cultivates sufficient imagination to visualize his role in the eyes of both man and God.

Before I can say anything sensible about the left fender on the chassis, I must revert to the Trinity. We earlier glimpsed the activity that from all eternity has swirled within the threeness of the one God: the constant and loving interchange of all good gifts. The City of God is the predestined extension of this sociability, with the doors open for all men and women who will consent to enter and take their serious part in the laughing game. The city of man is the provisional, very imperfect, but utterly essential approximation of the City of God.

The clue to the meaning of the assembly-line worker's job can be found only by looking at the city of man —at society as a whole—and seeing which of its activities are the strongest echoes of the dance of interchange within the depths of the blessed Trinity. The resemblance is strongest when self-sufficiency is least cherished. The ideal is a game in which gifts are constantly given and received; but one does not give directly to the person from whom one receives.

The pattern must be as complex as possible. For example, I teach college students, and assist week-ends at the Episcopal Church in my college town. Elsewhere, someone whom I shall probably never meet is writing textbooks that my children study in school. All of us are protected by aviators stationed in some frozen wasteland. Meanwhile, the assembly-line worker is screwing the left fender onto an automobile that may be bought by the physician who makes a house call on the writer of textbooks.

Viewed thus, there are few activities more meaningful than screwing the left fender onto a chassis that pauses a carefully timed moment. But it requires imagination to see the luminous way in which the most routine activities are mirrors of the City of God, and beyond that, mirrors of the divine interchange of courtesies within the lively eternity of the Trinity.

It requires imagination; without imagination and a sense of luminous wonder, the people suffocate. Only

with these additional pairs of eyes can one deeply perceive mankind's interchange of services and favors—not
merely across space but also across time. All prehistory
and history are part of one common enterprise. A carpenter, helping to build the great fourteenth-century
lantern tower of Ely Cathedral, could look down and
study the Norman work done by ancestors of his, seven
or eight generations earlier. The system of government
that safeguards my freedom has roots in the period that
men dare call "dark"; the blood of its martyrs has nour-
ished it, and will continue to nourish it. Language itself
is an enterprise shared across the centuries. I am able
to say what cries out in me to be said because the pa-
gans of northwest Europe brought their tongue to Brit-
ain fifteen hundred years ago, and it became crossed
with the Latin of churchmen and scholars, and the
French of the Norman adventurers. Along the way,
Chaucer and Shakespeare and T. S. Eliot and generation after generation of nameless men and women have
worked at perfecting the tool I use. It is as though every musician at birth found a Stradivarius violin thrust
free into his hands.

The left fender is not only dignified and meaningful;
it is exciting. It is part of the interchange of gifts in the
present moment, and it is linked with a continuing in-

terchange across the centuries from the first cart to the latest motor vehicle. But—as I had to confess—this sense of wonder does not come easily, either to factory workers or to those who play a dominant role in shaping the mentality of our period. If imagination and wonder are temporarily dormant, what remains?

Christ remains. As usual, He remains the most realistic source of strength and hope, here as in everything. We saw how Christ has redeemed pain and suffering. Tears of sorrow and cries of pain are links with One Who experienced in full depth the meaning of joy and the meaning of agony. In the same way, Christ has redeemed work; He redeemed it by doing it. He was a carpenter, skilled in wood and saws and hammers and nails. A carpenter works with both his mind and his body. No work can ever be free henceforth from that touch. The mind working or the hands working—these are following a way that Christ has explored, redeemed, and made radiant with His blessing and presence. Just as every supper consumed to the glory of God is an echo of one Last Supper, so every act of work rightly undertaken issues from the one carpentry shop.

⇶ XIII ⇷

Finders and Makers

THE CURSE can be partly lifted from work, so that it becomes an obedient and even joyful sharing with others and with Christ. But joyful or not, it is necessary; to live, we must have our daily bread. For most of us, that means earning it.

Man, however, does not live by bread alone. Christ and the anthropologists agree. No society has been discovered whose members do not spend part of their time at activities that have no obvious connection with bread-making and breadearning. There is always leisure to sing, to dance, to carve a design on the handle of the hunting knife, to tattoo the skin. Nor was the cave man an exception; at least fifteen thousand years ago he was decorating his walls with paintings that few art students can equal today.

Always, of course, there is the question, in dealing with another society, whether activities that we should call "art" were meant as art. Perhaps the cave drawings were magic symbols to aid the hunt; the song that the anthropologist hears some islander singing may have been intended to make yams grow or women conceive. Not every nation divides its pursuits into as many neat compartments as we do. But it is interesting that we find very little difficulty in responding to the cave drawings *as art,* and that we soon learn to enjoy "primitive" music for its own musical worth. Though to the cave man and some contemporary primitives the arts may be more than mere art, they are probably not less.

Art is everywhere. Go into the poorest mountaineer house, where the struggle for existence is bitter indeed, and you are almost certain to find several of the arts represented. The pictures on the wall may be clipped from magazines, and represent nothing finer than sentimental sunsets and boys with dogs—but they are there, nailed to the wall. The father has his banjo or guitar, and if he has not succumbed to the radio, he knows an impressive repertoire of folk songs and ballads, and their literary and musical worth is so great that Ph.D.'s come to collect and publish them. His wife triples the time it takes to make a quilt in order to produce beautiful patchwork.

Another thing impresses me. In Florence the Medicis no longer ponder poison, and no one assassinates a

Medici in the cathedral; nor is a troublesome reformer burned in the public square on charges of heresy. But the city remains an interlocking gallery of paintings and sculpture, and on the Ponte Vecchio the timeless crafts-men sell silverware and jewelry so exquisite that it escapes altogether from the framework of time. Passions have seethed and gone; the passion of art remains. In Scotland, the armed bands no longer pour down from the dark hills to the war wail of bagpipes, but on the esplanade by Edinburgh Castle you can see, at an occa-sional sunset, the drummers and kilted pipers playing and marching in a pattern as pure and perfect as the Russian ballet. Violence and terror have been transfig-ured into art, and the art remains. 74382

But this is not a book on esthetics. Our question here is simply: do the arts have anything to do with God?

Think of the piece of music that has most persistently haunted you over a period of years. If you are totally deaf to the voice of music, a poem or painting or statue or building will do—but music is best, for it is the most perfect of the arts, so perfect that by comparison a poet or a painter is a stammerer.

Can you put into words what this piece of music does for and in and to you? If you can, you have lost it. The secret of music is that it cannot be uttered except in music. Words can do little more than phrase a few clumsy clues: "It makes me feel that I am outside myself"—"It sweeps me along into another world"—"It takes all my griefs, cleanses them, and makes them beautiful."

Music—like every other art—sums up ordinary life by going beyond it. Just as we never see ourselves truly until we are mirrored in the eyeballs of Christ, so we do not understand and fully experience the fact and depth of everyday life until it is mirrored, transcended, and given back to us by someone competent for so delicate and demanding a mission.

The man who composed the piece of music that haunts you was a voyager on an expedition vaster and more uncertain than that of Columbus. His universe is one of an infinite number of worlds to be explored. The supply will not run out for him, nor for the composers who carry on after him the work of exploration. One world that he explores and maps he may call "Symphony in ————"; another simply "Melody in ————." There are worlds of magnitudes to be explored. But he can record them because he has been there.

There is another way, though, that this can be said. I have been talking as though the composer were an explorer, a "finder," bringing back reports of his discoveries. But you may prefer to think of him as a "maker." If you regard him thus, you will say that he invents the worlds he offers to you. For example, after he has composed his "Symphony in ————" it is as though a new star or a new solar system had suddenly appeared on the photographic plates of the astronomer.

Perhaps the composer is both a "finder" and a "maker." Perhaps, in some non-Aristotelian logic of heaven, the two are really one. This paradoxical possibility should not startle any Christian. He already believes in a God Who is simultaneously one and three; a God Who gives us free will and yet somehow weaves our free acts into that total pattern of events that was in the Designer's mind before the foundations of the world were laid.

If you prefer to think of the composer as a "maker," who brings into being a world or a series of worlds that would not exist except for him, then he does this as God's junior partner. To the composer has been delegated the creation of the music that is needed for the fullness of God's creation. Consider Bach, whose music has the reach and the depth of Shakespeare transfigured into music. You can say that Bach's work came into existence because God is such a fountainhead of song that

He passed along the capacity for song with the rest of His image when He created the human race, and out of His love of song He also made a world with horsetails, maple wood, and the other essentials for musical instruments. Bach therefore simply continued the work of creation that God had begun. What he added to creation he laid at the feet of God, saying, "I have made this for You."

But if you prefer to think of a composer as a "finder," you will say that Bach did not create anything; he merely captured it. He discovered worlds of music that sing eternally in the ear of God; discovered them, and translated them into black marks on paper, so that the music that is God's delight can be man's also. It was a sort of incarnation—first the eternal music in God's ear, then the explorer, the black marks on paper, and finally the vibrations set in motion by the skilled hands of musicians.

It does not greatly matter. Bach does. However we express it, the composer—by continuing God's creation or exploring it—reveals to us the dimensions and depths of that universe, its worlds beyond worlds, its songs that sounded or were waiting to sound before God sang the first atoms into being.

⇻≫ XIV ≪⇺

The Beauty and Holiness
of Thought

WHEN in 1543 Copernicus published *De Revolutioni-bus Orbium Coelestium,* he was unable to prove em-pirically that the earth revolves around the sun. Even today, despite all that the telescope and other scientific apparatus have contributed, the empirical proof of the Copernican theory is not in itself decisive. Copernicus believed—and we believe—in his system for a quite dif-ferent reason, which must presently be examined.

It is essential that we be fair toward the men who in 1543 were not immediately convinced. If one forgets everything he learned in astronomy class and simply observes the world as it appears, the obvious conclusion is in favor of Ptolemy, not Copernicus. The earth seems huge and solid; the stars and planets seem frail and in-consequential. The sun clearly "rises" and "sets"; it and the other heavenly bodies evidently move in complex patterns around the earth, which alone stays still.

Hardheaded common sense was against Copernicus in his own time, *and still is.* It requires a real suppression of common sense to think of this massive earth as something other than the center of the universe. Yet Ptolemy was not supported simply by the common sense of the average citizen. Even the science of Copernicus' time did not require the new theory. Every celestial phenomenon then known could be handled by the Ptolemaic system, and the latter was equally accurate in its predictions of astronomical events.

It appears, therefore, that even if theological and philosophic anxieties had been totally lacking, there were yet weighty reasons—which a "realistic" modern can appreciate—for deciding, "These new ideas go against common sense—and any way, *they aren't necessary.*"

In truth, Copernicus had only one compelling reason for insisting that the earth moves around the sun: it makes elegant mathematics. Instead of requiring the eighty epicycles of the Ptolemaic system, he could explain all the known phenomena with thirty-four.

Copernicus was like an art critic gazing at two paintings of the same landscape. One is a typical nineteenth century oil color, with every square inch of the canvas crisscrossed by dozens of fussy brush strokes. The other is a Japanese water color, in which a few bold strokes are able to capture the entire scene. The critic votes for the economy and elegance of the second painting; Copernicus wanted his mathematics economical and elegant.

Modern science rests on esthetics. Its "law of parsimony"—the preference for theories as simple as possible, that will adequately cover as much territory as possible —is based on the unprovable assumption that reality is elegant. Behind that assumption—though not always consciously recognized—is faith in an elegant God, Who operates with bold, purposeful strokes. Copernicus was one of the pioneers in his insistence on economy and elegance as touchstones for testing the hypotheses of science. Science has followed his intuition.

It is a curious coincidence—or perhaps none at all— that the greatest mathematical mind since Newton was possessed by a man who was also a gifted amateur violinist. When advancing years and failing health made it impossible for Einstein to trudge on foot through rain and snow to the Institute for Advanced Study at Princeton; when he had to consent to be driven in a car; when finally that mind of clarity, depth, and singular purity came to an earthly end, with a few German phrases muttered to a nurse who understood no German—when this mind, God-like in its integrity, childlike in its innocence, ceased to labor, something of surpassing beauty left this earth, and left it shrunken and impoverished. To the last he sought God by seeking to find Him revealed in the most elegant mathematics conceivable. He died without knowing whether empirical evidence would ever vindicate his Unified Field Theory, in which he attempted to unite in one formula the forces of the microcosmic world and those of the macrocosm.

The scientist and the artist have in common their intuition of underlying elegance; they are also parallel voyagers beyond common sense, seeking that which will both transcend and illuminate ordinary experience. Certainly, much art at once removes me from the everyday world and helps me to understand it better; much science outrages common sense (as when it tells me that the table at which I am working is mostly empty space), and simultaneously it helps me to understand better the things I have taken for granted: such as a tomato, which is revealed with a genealogy to mock the recorded lineage of any king.

Indeed, the more one thinks about it, the more difficult it becomes to separate the functions of scientist and artist. But there is one obvious difference: good art does not grow old; good science (good at its time) does. The poetry of Gerard Manley Hopkins, composed in the nineteenth century, is as fresh and meaningful as any written today; the lyrics from the Greek anthology are fresher than most of the current popular songs. But the science of the nineteenth century has been corrected and modified in so many ways that a freshman beginning his first science course in college has no need to select one dealing solely with "nineteenth century science." Whatever was true in the science of that period is retained by contemporary science; what was false or inadequate may properly be left to the historians of science. As for the science of Aristotle's time, it is shot so full of errors that anyone studying it alone, without the corrective of modern science, would be led into grave errors.

Science is a cumulative enterprise; each generation of scientists is free to pick and choose from the scientific theories produced by even the greatest scientists of earlier generations. Whatever appears useful is retained; the rest is brushed aside. But the arts are very different. We cannot say that Eliot incorporates the best of Shakespeare and renders Shakespeare unnecessary; for that matter, we cannot say that Shakespeare completes and supersedes Chaucer. It seems that in any art there is an unlimited number of worlds and universes to be explored and recorded; or, if you prefer the other way of viewing it, there are countless potential worlds and universes waiting for some artist to love them into being and offer them at the feet of God. However you phrase it, it means that good art does not become mediocre with the passage of time; what is once good—truly good —is eternally good.

Yet the ways in which the artist and the scientist differ are less important than the many ways in which they are one. Both consciously or unconsciously seek the glory of God, in order to declare it—through poems, paintings, music, mathematics, formulae. Both seek God's glory because they bear within themselves His image—which, as in all men, needs God's restoring hand to heal its wounds, yet is able to whisper, nag, and encourage them on by saying, "Look, see what I have done. Keep going. There is more to see . . . and more."

We are condemned to failure if we try to separate the scientist and the artist by saying that one works with the rational mind and the other with intuition. Both are defamed by such a line of demarcation, for it suggests that science and art flourish only when those who practice one or the other consent to be less than full men.

Scientists are not mere atom-counters and syllogistic machines. This may be the conviction of logical positivists and sidewalk scientists, but no real scientist fits the barren stereotype. Real science is rich and juicy. The scientist wakes up suddenly, or is surprised by voices in the air while walking to work. Lights flash in his brain. He entertains ideas wilder than those of playful children. He becomes cold-blooded only when he tests his ideas.

The artist also hears voices, and sees lights flash. And he too puts the sober mind to work at understanding and imposing form on the slithering masses of intuitively perceived material. "I feel like a carpenter when I sit down to write a poem," a distinguished poet told me. I think I know what he means. It is a rare writer who can take the flash of inspiration and convert it into words without going through an intellectual process as rigorous as that of a scientist setting up an experiment to test an hypothesis. If anyone doubts this, he has only to look at the work-sheets of Keats or Yeats and compare them with their published poems.

But the finished products? Does the scientist's verified theory induce intellectual assent, and the poet's poem evoke emotion? Again, that is too simple. Take some completely worked out system of cosmology, one that offers at least a plausible guess as to the origin, structure, and functioning of the universe. Who can separate the intellectual satisfaction of the student from the sense of awe and wonder which arises at his being given this elegant hint of one way that all visible things may relate themselves to one another?

Now take a poem. Here is one, written by Sir Thomas Wyatt at about the time that Copernicus was bidding the earth move round the sun:

> They flee from me that sometime did me seek,
> With naked foot stalking in my chamber.
> I have seen them gentle, tame, and meek,
> That now are wild, and do not remember
> That some time they put themselves in danger
> To take bread at my hand; and now they range,
> Busily seeking with a continual change.
>
> Thanked be fortune, it hath been otherwise
> Twenty times better; but once, in speciall,
> In thin array, after a pleasant guise,
> When her loose gown from her shoulders did fall,
> And she me caught in her arms long and small.
> Therewith all sweetly did me kiss,
> And softly said, Dear heart, how like you this?
>
> It was no dream; I lay broad waking.
> But all is turned, thorough my gentleness,
> Into a strange fashion of forsaking;
> And I have leave to go of her goodness,

And she also to use newfangleness.
But since that I so kindely am served,
I fain would know what she hath deserved.*

Until God abolishes the distinction between men and women, or alternatively subjects them to some process of psychological conditioning so that they will automatically be faithful to each other, this poem will have the power to summon up complex clusters of emotions and memories: strange encounters, sudden joy, casual commitment, civilized departure, the dreamlike quality of the whole thing, the implied passage of time that makes it less likely to happen again.

But reread the poem. It is no mere invitation to emotional indulgence; it has an intellectual austerity. Note the extreme accuracy of the basic comparison: it is as though a half-tame deer from an English park had wandered into the poet's room, "with naked foot," "stalking," for the time being "gentle, tame, and meek," and had paused "to take bread" from his hand. But a deer is free to come and go. It can revert to the wild state, or it may stalk elsewhere and seek bread at other hands. But the poem vibrates far beyond this. It explores the

* Quoted from Mark Van Doren, *Introduction to Poetry*, The Dryden Press, Inc., New York, 1951, pp. 34–5. The version given here differs slightly from the more familiar one, first published in *Tottell's Miscellany*, which represents the attempt of the good Tottell to smooth out the apparent—but probably deliberate—roughness of Wyatt's verse.

mysterious interplay of attraction and repulsion between a man and a woman: the mutual need, the
mutual mystery, the leaps of understanding, and the
subsequent doubt that any understanding ever existed.

I have still barely grazed the surface of this poem.
But I think I have made my point: here is a catalyst for
the emotions, and at the same time the most rigorous
intellectual accuracy. The mind and the spinal cord are
equally responsive to it. And I find the same thing to be
true of the pivotal scientific hypotheses and theories.

In both the great scientist and the great artist, intel-
lect nourishes intuition, and intuition nourishes intel-
lect. This should not startle anyone who has pondered
the meaning of Christ. In Him we see the incarnation
of God's Logos—the Word, the eternal reason and ra-
tionality within the Godhead. But the story of Christ is
also a love story. Because of God's love for His creation,
He came down from heaven, to an earth that is not
heaven.

Christ is both reason and love made visible. He reveals that God is reason, yet more than reason. We,
bearing that image, are reason and more than reason.

But God is not less than reason; we do not compli-
ment Him when we make a cult of "blind faith." Next
to the capacity for receiving and giving love, the power

of reason is as astonishing a gift as any that the rational and loving God has bestowed on us. There are not many better temples than the scholar's study and the scientist's laboratory.

⇢≫ XV ≪⇠

Basic Training for the Love of God

You can find out some of the things that exist, and their meaning, through the sciences and the arts, but there are additional ways. One is to fall in love.

Romantic love is fraught with perils and full of promises. Nowhere is the need greater for clear thinking and clear language. One must steer between the Scylla of cheap sentimentality and thrills, and the Charybdis of those cold and worried sociological treatises on marital adjustment. Fortunately this can be done, and often is done.

First, let us strip Scylla of her sentiment. We can begin by pointing out that although romantic love actually exists, and is frequent and important, this does not imply any doctrine that "there is only one woman in the world for me." The experience of romantic love can be repeated. That two people have been in love with each other does not incapacitate them from falling in love with someone else. Nor does romantic love necessarily lead to marriage; sometimes it should not. Two people may be deeply in love, yet hopelessly separated by temperamental and psychological differences. And finally, when marriage does follow, the special kind of vision that romantic love imparts does not necessarily remain constant. It may flicker and come and go; it may fade away completely, and be replaced by a quieter, less beatific vision. This does not disprove the original vision, nor does it annul the continued validity and inner reality of the marriage.

These many negations do not compel us to steer toward cold Charybdis. The experience of romantic love, whether it lasts a lifetime or ten minutes, is one of the plain facts with which we must reckon, if we are to make sense of life. It is yet another door suddenly opening.

What happens is that the lover sees his beloved as she essentially is, and she sees him as he essentially is. What they essentially are is not what they are at the moment; that is what the camera records. But to take its verdict as final is like regarding the smudge on a woman's cheek, when she stands up beside the stove, as final.

The lover sees not merely the transient woman, but the eternal woman half hidden—the woman she will be in God's good time if she consents to His plans for her redemption and glorification.

It is as though the lover looks backward and forward at the same time. His beloved is in Eden, and Paradise has not been lost; she is standing among the shining saints in the final times. Therefore his knowledge is true knowledge; it is knowledge of what God intends as truth for this woman. In so far as she sees her lover in this same manner, her knowledge also is true. And each of them, having seen God's truth in one face, is better enabled to catch glimpses of it in all faces.

When romantic love does lead to marriage, the devil immediately pricks up his pointed ears. He comes cheerfully to any wedding. He has already walked beside the lovers during their moonlight strolls, hoping to mingle his whispers with their own; and he will not forsake them after they have spoken their promises at the altar.

In general, the devil operates on the assumption that the more beautiful and God-blessed anything is, the more useful it can prove to him. Reasoning thus, he works to persuade the husband and wife that marriage is so complete a fulfillment as to obviate the need for any other temple than their home. He teaches each to regard the other as god enough. If he succeeds, they begin—quite literally—to "idolize" each other.

This form of religion—like many other forms—delights the devil more than any amount of atheism. He agrees with the Bible, which solemnly warns time and again against idolatry, but is almost silent in regard to atheism. And the devil prefers that idolatry be on a high level. He knows that a confirmed alcoholic may some day wake up in revulsion and join Alcoholics Anonymous. But if a man's wife truly reflects the radiance and glory of her Creator, if she deserves a love separated only by a hair's-breadth from idolatry, can her husband be expected to arise some morning with disgust in his heart and organize Idolaters Anonymous?

"God, Thou art here—and this is Thine—but this is not Thou." These three cries need to be uttered often and with equal emphasis; they are passwords to spiritual health—and not alone in marriage. The nature lover needs to say them to nature, the social reformer to his work of reform.

"This is not Thou—my wife or my husband is not God. This is another finite and inevitably sinful creature who shares my life with me." But—"Thou art here —and this is Thine. In this love, which Thou hast made possible, this love that exists because Thou hast created the one who shares my life with me, I am preparing

[117]

myself for the time when a still greater love—an inconceivably greater love—will engulf the two of us."

Love God and laugh at the devil. Assuming that a husband and wife obey these twin commandments, and thereby keep their love for each other this side of idolatry, what can Christian marriage do to bring them nearer to God? Certainly, wedlock is one of God's preferred schools, for He sees to it that most of us enroll as pupils.

If the marriage is based on romantic love, it offers further opportunity for each to see the other as he essentially and potentially is, with the dew of Eden still fresh, and time in its fullness of redeemed splendor. I have already spoken of this—the deep, clear vision.

But marriage offers also the gift of God-blessed sex. Sex, with thanks to God and to His glory, can make of marriage a school of reverence for the whole material universe that God has created. Here, between a man and a woman, is a love both physical and spiritual. For a man to tell his wife that he loves her spirit and then end the sentence with a period is blasphemy against both her and the God Who lovingly created more than spirit.

Love, which claims both body and spirit, is a human clue to the meaning of the sacraments. The lover, when he stops to think about it, will see how reasonable it is that water can mean a real death and a real rebirth, and that Christ embodies Himself in bread and wine. He will recognize, too, that whereas the familiar sacraments are the Mount Everests of the sacramental landscape, there are other mountains and foothills. Something of the sacramental—less charted but undeniable—is to be found in sticks and stones and horses and birds and the meetings of the city council.

Marriage is also a small-scale demonstration of the truth that you must die in order to live, and that only after you cease to be merely yourself will you begin to be really yourself. That the "one flesh" may come into being, the husband dies to himself, the wife to herself. From double surrender and double death, "one flesh" is born. But within the unity of the new being, a twin resurrection is made manifest. The husband and wife, without ceasing to be one flesh, become more profoundly than ever themselves. This is a partial though admittedly imperfect allegory for the Christian experience of conversion. The person who dies to himself, and then rises from this particular death, with Christ as the new life within him, is yet not absorbed by Christ. For the first time he is truly himself, for his true self is liberated and revealed by the Christ Who dwells within.

Finally—but not last in order of importance—there is the gift of children. Here is a miracle more astonishing than anything Christ did with loaves and fishes. Here God has delegated His creativity so that its joy may be intimately shared. God, the angels in heaven, the parents and their families and friends, all are permitted a full share of rejoicing when a child is born. Here is love incarnate.

At the moment of the miracle, when a new life is thrust into the hands of the two human beings chosen to cherish and guide it, a flood of new knowledge enters the father and mother. They know intuitively that God's love and His creativity are as inseparable within His own being as are the body and spirit of love. They know now and at last what it means when we say that God is a Father, forever seeking every prodigal son. They comprehend—perhaps for the first time—the depth of the love that moved God when He sent His only-begotten Son to endure all that was required to be endured, for the salvation of the prodigal sons.

⇛ XVI ⇚

The Scattered Fellowship

SOLITARY confinement is the ultimate punishment that any warden can inflict on the recalcitrant: more dreaded than the lash, more destructive of hope and sanity.

The hermit and the happy castaway are so tiny a percentage of mankind that they merely dramatize by contrast the desperate need we have of one another.

Yet a man may move every day in swarms of people, many of whom he knows by name, and still be lonely; many vigorous extroverts are desperately lonely. It is not simply the presence of other human flesh that banishes loneliness; it is understanding and being understood, loving and being loved.

The meeting of two personalities can exist in all degrees of completeness. When—on rare occasions—I attend a professional conference of literature teachers, we make ready contact: Shakespeare and Faulkner are sufficient introductions. But longer acquaintance often makes for less understanding. We discover the many ways in which people in the same profession may utterly lack contact once they talk something other than "shop."

Still one should give thanks to Shakespeare and Faulkner. They are better than nothing; they are at least a beachhead of understanding. Almost anything can be a beachhead. A few years ago I learned to play the Elizabethan flute that is called by the confusing name of "recorder." What one can do on so simple an instrument is limited, and so is my talent; but even so, the most astonishing results have ensued. I now find myself feeling a new rapport with musicians—the real ones—and with music-store clerks, publishers of music, all sorts of musical amateurs, and amateurs of every other kind. More than this, the barriers of time are neatly abolished. When I play the music, say, of Corelli or Purcell or Mozart, I sense a gradual revelation: they reveal themselves to me in proportion as I give myself to their music.

But all these are partial ways of meeting. I have found another remedy against loneliness—one that offers greater knowing. This is the scattered fellowship of those who meet in God. The fellowship does not have the same boundaries as the visible Church. The latter contains many who are accidentally there; the fellow-ship embraces many who ought to be there but are not.

When I first discovered the scattered fellowship, I was puzzled—perhaps a little troubled—to observe that some of its members had never belonged, and had no intention of belonging, to the Christian Church. They were, in certain cases, members of the other great religions; more frequently they were spiritual individualists, unwilling to accept any existing system of religion. And yet, in their lives and sometimes in their faces, I detected the unmistakable working of God; and when we talked together, I found the instant understanding that exists between those who are centered in one common Center.

I see now that I was making God too small. I believe today, more profoundly than I did then, that the Apostles' Creed and the Nicene Creed, as summaries of Christian belief, are true in the same way that the multiplication table is true. They would be true if no one in the world believed they were true. But I failed to realize that a God as all-present and all-powerful and all-loving as the one proclaimed by the historic creeds is a God entitled to pick any lock and batter down any door. The fact that the creeds are true is no reason for assuming that God can and will work only through

[123]

those who believe them to be true. God roams; He breaks; He enters; He is not above using an alias; He chooses and stations His witnesses where He will.

Once you begin to look for these witnesses, you find them everywhere. A casual word on a train, a glance at the book someone is reading, a stranger's reaction to a momentary situation, even the impersonal proceedings of a business meeting—the quiet clues are everywhere. If you follow them up, you may in half an hour find yourself with a kind of understanding that you have not achieved in ten years with your next-door neighbor.

These friendships—perhaps barely begun and seemingly terminated by separation—are almost impervious to time and distance. You can meet once and briefly. For five years, no letter is exchanged. You meet again. You take up from where you left off . . . or at a point beyond, if both of you have been growing in parallel ways.

The scattered fellowship laughs at the usual sociological barriers: class, education, income, nationality, race. It is not so much that each member, mindful of his duty, struggles to transcend the barriers; rather that the barriers are lightly brushed aside, as though a man were hurrying to catch an essential train and murmured "Excuse me" as he gently pushed his way forward.

As you go further into the mysteries of the fellow-ship, you begin to see all other relationships in the light of it. Superficial, gregarious friendship shrinks before your eyes. Other relationships, perhaps troubled and never even called "friendship" in your mind, suddenly detach themselves from the confused matrix of their setting, and you see them for what they are—manifestations of the latent brotherhood.

God made this world and sustains it. But next to God, I suspect it is the scattered fellowship that does most to keep the very globe from splitting into as many frag-ments as there are human beings.

PART THREE

Discovery

⇛ XVII ⇚

Stained Glass and the Light
of the Sun

I will tell you a parable.

I once made a trip to Chartres. As I descended from the train, I saw in the distance the twin towers of the cathedral. The mild sun of northern France was shining, clearly but without flamboyance. The scene before me was one of soft grays and browns.

I walked to the cathedral and went inside. I looked up at one of the windows. The sun was shining through it, and at last I knew the nature of sunlight. Sunlight is the blue, the red, the green of the stained glass at Chartres. I had never before known the color of sunlight.

Ordinarily sunlight appears colorless, because it is too full of color for our eyes to see that it is colored. Sunlight is not the absence of color; it is the fullness of color—all the colors of the spectrum in their purity and united. To see sunlight as it really is I had to go to Chartres Cathedral, for there the stained glass that faith bequeathed to faith is able to separate sunlight into blue and red and green, and let me see sunlight as it is.

I looked from one window to another. I knew then that heaven has to exist. Heaven is where God's light can be steadily seen for what it is: where one beholds the glory of red and blue and green.

Ordinarily our eyes cannot or will not behold the glory. They see God's light as colorless, and therefore do not see it. But God is merciful and patient. When least expected He intervenes in my life or yours, as decisively as when He led the Israelites out of Egypt through the Red Sea. He makes blind eyes to see. For an instant we behold the glory of blue and green and red. The door has quickly opened and we see the light within.

This is the meaning of the long moments, the quick eternities that waylay us; in them we see the light as it is. We are being prepared for that time beyond time when we shall be able to look steadily upon the red, the blue, and the green, and not be blinded by the un-created glory.

⇢⇢⇢ XVIII ⇠⇠⇠

The Shadow

But what have the splendor of Chartres and the intuition of God's prismatic light to do with the muted voyage of exploration in which we recently engaged?

We found no way to pry the door open, no way to command that apparently colorless light be red, blue, and green. But then we did not expect to find a way. The moments of vision remain what they have been— gifts of grace, freely given at times and places selected by the Giver.

Nonetheless, I end the voyage moderately satisfied. Everything I discovered was one degree removed from the primal splendor, but one degree is still not far from the source. By taking the unsought moments of insight as touchstones, I discovered that the most humdrum activities and settings bear unmistakable though quieter witness to the radiant God Who is their ground and their goal. Nothing remained commonplace; everywhere were candid hints of the God who is God of all and in all.

Perhaps my eyes are not strong enough to bear the constant glory; God mercifully subdues His brightness most of the time. Perhaps this is true; but it does not matter. I have beheld the glory in quick moments; I have discerned its reflected and muted splendor in many landscapes and common deeds; God in His own way will make my eyes at last able to behold the constant glory without flinching.

I come back from the voyage, convinced that nothing is commonplace. The distinction between everyday fact and miracle has begun to break down in my mind. The tomato in my hand is as much a miracle as water turned into wine or Lazarus restored to his family; my work, no matter how dull it sometimes seems, ceases to be dull when I see it as my coöperation with a creative God, and my contribution to that gay interchange of favors and services that constitutes the pastime of the City of God.

All this knowledge is very great gain. God's world is bigger, brighter, and more inclusive than I had realized, and it extends to tiny and transient details. Nothing is too small or too big for Him. I believe that henceforth

I shall be better able to think of God as the most important fact in every landscape, every activity.

I look at the world about me and all the things that are, and I see new goodness in them. The sun is shining brightly, and there are no shadows anywhere.

Yet, in this very moment of deepening contentment, when God is so omnipresent that every blade of grass and every act of labor is a kind of creed to affirm His presence, I become conscious of something else. Despite God's presence, I am afraid.

I become aware of myself. Here am I, on a small sphere that seems each day more like a particle of dust. Astronomy builds new telescopes to humble it; supersonic flight engirdles it; desperate men play with poisonous toys that could smother all green and living things from its surface.

But here am I, on a globe that is still green and blue and brown; a globe that faithfully turns on its axis every twenty-four hours and continues its yearly trip around the sun. It is a speck of dust yet one teeming with life; I can scarcely descend deep enough or climb high enough to escape the companionship of life. This only makes bleaker the light-years that separate me from every other planet on which I might plausibly hope to find rational life. If, on some other planet circling round

some other star, men not too different from me are looking into space for companionship, it does neither them
nor me any good; we cannot meet.

I am here on the earth. Deep in the rocks are the
bones of creatures who once walked or waddled on the
surface, or flitted above it. The campus of Beloit College
is dotted with Indian mounds in some of which are skel-
etons as old as Chaucer. In the mild spring weather I
can see students, two by two, sitting on the mounds,
laughing, unmindful of the dead. At the edge of town
is a more recent cemetery where the bodies of men and
women I once knew are now a few feet below the green
face of the earth.

With the precision of a beautifully made clock, this
globe on which I live is aging me. Each revolution
round the sun, each daily rotation, brings me nearer to
the time when I must descend from green to black.

It is a very lonely feeling to think of this—to know
that the green earth will continue its accurate turning, its scheduled circuit around the sun; to know that
I can be so alive today that the world seems to exist
because of me, and know at the same time how momentary an inhabitant I am. The unborn are waiting for me
to yield my place.

As I think about it, the very light of the sun seems an

illusion—a beautiful dream rather than a warm reality. From the far reaches of interstellar space, darkness rushes down and eddies about me. I am surrounded by darkness; I cannot see. I know now that no cross is required to wring from my lips the cry, *Eli, Eli, lama sabachthani?*

It is a very deep darkness, and a darkness that mocks. All that I remember from my voyage of exploration seems laughable and flimsy and forced, like the imaginary playmates that lonesome children create for themselves. Darkness, I tell myself, this darkness is the truth. This is where I have always been, but now at last I will admit that it is darkness.

A voice speaks from the darkness. "Why have I forsaken you? I have not. Here I am."

"Who are you?" I ask.

"One who spoke the words that you have spoken."

"I cannot see you. The darkness is too deep."

"Do not try to see me," the voice continues. "Merely listen. This darkness is the shadow of death. Death is a shadow now. He was not a shadow when I met him, and when I cried out with the words you uttered. I have met death and left him the shadow of death."

The voice dies away. The darkness folds back and is gone. The sun shines very brightly. I see no one.

⇒⇒ XIX ⇐⇐

Shadows

THOUGH the sun is now shining everywhere, I do not
doubt that the shadow will return, and return again.
But let it come; for this long moment I am free of it,
and the cold desolation has left me. When it comes once
more, I think I can meet it better.

My mind turns to the brave men who have faced
death with no hint of the knowledge that Christ won
between a Friday and a Sunday. The folklore of the
world bears witness of what many expected to find: a
pale and idiot eternity of gibbering spirits and decayed
lives in some underworld from which the sun, even the
gods, were excluded. I see that Christ is not merely the
second Adam but the second Aeneas—one who visited
the departed and prepared a way for all who must follow; one who explored and found that God will not die
from my life when I die. What Christ found on the
other side of death He could not put into words that I

can understand now; but what He found I find in Christ.

The sun is shining brightly. Any tree, any stone may suddenly open wide and let me inside. This landscape is filled with hopeful rumors. My eye travels around, eagerly. But a slow change begins. The more my attention strains toward first one object and then another, and the harder I try to project myself within it, the more mottled the sunlight becomes. It does not seem to be penetrating everywhere.

There are dark and half-hidden pockets of ground—spaces filled with shadows. Here and there I think I see also the mouths of caves. Perhaps I have been trying too hard to see sunlight everywhere. Perhaps these shadows, which pockmark the landscape, are not mere imperfections in my vision; they are real, they are *there*. There are more shadows than the shadow of death.

I look up; no cloud intervenes between the earth and the sun. But the shadows remain, all round me, and some of them are beginning to join and thicken.

As I stop to think about it, every good and God-blessed thing is subject to darkness. Take a human body, as beautiful and marvelously precise a machine as any designer could produce. It seems the violin for God's bow, so exquisitely is it built. But consider the same body when blood vessels harden or a cancer spreads its fingers; here is darkness—not the illusion of darkness, but the reality.

Or pick up the evening newspaper and read the head-lines: murder, arson, robbery, divorce, a report on how much new radioactivity has been released into the essential atmosphere. When I study history, I do not find that mankind was wiser in the past, but merely less competent to do evil on a grand scale: the cave man smashed skulls instead of cities.

Then I think of the way of two human beings with each other. Consider marriage. See how easily the two inhabitants of Eden can will their exile; how soon the dark blotches of misunderstanding can come between them. It is easy for their friends to say that Eden was never more than a soft compound of moonlight and music. But its passing can leave two mortals drawn up behind the high barricades of their separate egos, each staring at a stranger.

My mind wanders to the world I know best: that of the classroom and faculty meeting. Here is a little universe dedicated to such virtues as intellectual integrity and objectivity. It is a privileged universe, partly protected from the savage pressures and distractions outside its boundaries. But I do not find that the campus is an intellectual Eden. If anyone doubts whether mankind is a fallen race, let him attend any faculty meeting anywhere and discover for himself how many egoistic cross-currents and antagonisms can masquerade under such impressive pseudonyms as "educational philosophy" and "academic policy."

But why should I turn sociologist in order to speak of shadows? I have enough inside me to darken the whole landscape if all my shadows chose to leave me and spread out. It is extraordinarily difficult to love God wholeheartedly; to love one's neighbor, even when he is lovable, is no easier. I know what I should do; there is nothing in the teachings of Christ that is clearer: go and love. But knowledge is one thing, deeds another. It seems as though I am two persons. One agrees with Christ and issues the appropriate orders. The other, with his own peculiar serenity, plays deaf, and continues to live as though my ego were the central point of the cosmos and all galaxies revolved around it.

But this does not exhaust my supply of shadows, nor does it include the darkest ones. Plain selfishness, crass lust, ruthless ambition: these are bad, but the hierarchy of shadows has space for darker shades. My truly black shadows overflow from me in those moments when I am suddenly convinced that "I'm actually making spiritual progress." This may be a time when prayer all at once ceases to be a duty and becomes a singing voice in counterpoint with my stumbling voice; it may be when I am carried away by my own eloquence in preaching a sermon; it can be five seconds after I have spontaneously behaved with humility or shown unpremeditated love toward a neighbor.

It is then that the displaced person, the devil, most boldly undertakes his work of shadow consolidation. In some simple disguise—perhaps dressed as one of the more devout members of the church—he congratulates me on my spiritual progress, and assures me that I am really getting to the point where I shall soon deserve God's sincere approval.

As he speaks, as I mentally nod agreement, the shadow of death rushes back from the reaches of interstellar space. It is darker and deeper than I remember it. The shadows remaining within me pour forth to meet it; the shadows from caves and hidden places in the landscape race together, and all shadows merge and swirl about me in one mass of dark shadow, like black water.

Then, as I watch, the sea of shadow begins to take on a geometrical shape. A long arm of blackness moves from my left to the horizon; another to my right; one ahead of me. I turn round. A fourth arm of darkness reaches to the horizon. I know now the shape of darkness.

In the center of darkness, where its four paths meet, I cannot see. But a voice says, "Here I am." It is the voice I heard before.

⇢⟫ XX ⟪⇠

God Is a Five-Act Drama

LET ME take stock. This voyage of exploration has been worth while. I found evidence that every activity and experience can supply hints—though subdued—of what the moments of the opening door more intensely reveal.

But now I am confused. Fears and darknesses keep crowding in; I must reckon with them, but I do not know for sure how I am to do this. Do they call into question the discoveries of the voyage? Do they annul the brief certainties of light that I have known in the long moments?

So far I have been as far as possible deliberately going it alone. I have learned much; but I have come to an end. If I am to learn more, it must be revealed to me with greater finality and clarity than I found in either the moments of the quickly opening door or in the discoveries of the voyage.

I must know more about God and His plans. This knowledge is available; it is summarized in the Bible, which is the inspired record and interpretation of the decisive deeds God has done and those He intends to do. In the Bible, if anywhere, I shall find the primal insights that will help me to make sense of all moments, luminous or muted, and see beyond them to the light that shines through them.

What is God doing? According to the Bible, He is writing a five-act play, producing it, and playing the principal role. Here is the plot.

Act One: Creation and Fall. When the curtain rises, there is nothing to be seen on the stage—unless the eye of the spirit can discern God. The universe exists only as a loving idea in the mind and heart of God. Then God brings the universe into being; wills it into existence, loves it into existence, sings it into existence— whatever the words. He creates a universe in which something akin to His own love can be experienced by other beings. Under His guidance, life moves from potentiality to reality. Countless forms are brought into being; man himself is finally revealed on the stage.*

* I am stating this as though there were a "time" when the universe did not exist, and then at a definite "time" God brought it into being. Such indeed may have been the case, though there is another scientific theory that the universe has always existed. If the latter is true, then God has been engaged in an eternal *process* of creation. The religious meaning of the Genesis story is the same in either case. Stated in mathematical symbols: God — Universe = God
Universe — God = 0

It is a universe whose perfection is intended by God. But something goes wrong; we can only speculate on the "what." It is hard to find a reason for sin, for sin is not reasonable. The ancient symbols of the inspired mythology are still best, for they have the greatest power of suggestion. On the stage, then, are Adam and Eve, knowing only good, for the world in which they live is wholly good. But a voice whispers. (You and I listen eagerly to that whisper, also; you and I are on the stage, here and all the way through the Bible.) They eat the forbidden fruit from the tree of the "knowledge of good and evil," hoping to become "as gods, knowing good and evil." They get more than they expected. God knows evil as an intellectual possibility; Adam and Eve learn to know it in their blood and their bones and in the rattle of death. Hastily clothed and banished from Paradise, they see the world as a thing turned hostile to them. And so the world indeed appears to anyone who has turned himself against God by trying to take His place.

As the curtain goes down, Cain is slaying his brother, and upstage men are making bricks with which to build the Tower of Babel.

Act Two: Reconstruction and Reëducation. The curtain rises on ruin and desolation. The broken bricks from the Tower of Babel—man's organized attempt to outdistance God—are scattered about in great heaps. The human race in little clusters is stumbling here and there, like the dazed survivors of an air raid. There is an uneasiness about the very sticks and stones and beasts of the field; something of the same disorder and distortion seems to have penetrated into them. But in the midst of the ruins, "the Lord had said unto Abram, Get thee out of thy country, and from thy kindred, and from thy father's house, unto a land that I will shew thee: And I will make of thee a great nation, and I will bless thee, and make thy name great; and thou shalt be a blessing: and I will bless them that bless thee, and curse him that curseth thee: and in thee shall all families of the earth be blessed."

Abram—later called Abraham—obeys God's call. With his obedience, God undertakes in earnest the reconstruction and reëducation of the human race; and beyond mankind, the reordering and renewal of His entire creation.

In this act of the drama, God establishes an experimental home for delinquent children. All the children are delinquent, but for His immediate purposes He singles out the Hebrews, a wandering desert people, as fiercely passionate as the burning heat of the desert, a people all fire and steel and hard strength. After He has reëducated and redirected them, He will be ready to deal directly with all humanity.

This second act is a very strange one. Through it stride the titanic figures of Abraham, Joseph, Moses, Joshua, David, and many others. Bloodshed, miracles, tortured despair, and exultant hope—all are intermingled in the successive tableaux.

But God's immediate aims are simple. He wants to reëducate the Hebrews so that they will know good *as good*. He teaches them plain facts: that there is one God and only one God, and that this one God is the sanction and jealous guardian of the moral order of the universe—an order as direct and sure in its operations as the law of gravitation. He promises that if they learn these few facts and live accordingly, He will protect them and see to their needs. If they do not . . .

Repeatedly the Hebrews rise to great heights of obedience; invariably they backslide; punishment falls on them; they repent; there is a fresh start; the same cycle starts all over again.

Gradually a deeper despair and a strange new hope arise. Voices cry out, "We do not have the strength to do this alone. Lord, send Thy anointed, Thy Messiah. Only He can do it for and with and in us."

Act Three: The Messiah. This is the act in which God is most obviously the leading member of the cast. And yet He is not at all obvious; if one were not informed by the program notes of His role, the fact might escape the spectator's attention. Even today, after more than a thousand years of Christmas carols, we are not accustomed to think of God as soon as we see a small baby in humble surroundings—say a stable. Nor does a carpenter's house suggest God's home. Neither, for that matter, does a criminal suffering some form of officially decreed death remind us instantly of God.

The Messiah is recognized only by those who see double; to their eyes He appears for what He is: the Son of God, the eternal Word of God, the Second Person of the everliving Trinity. Here is God come down from heaven, for us men and for our salvation.

Act Four: The Church. This is the act in which we are living, and is therefore a bewildering one. On the one hand Christ has defeated sin and death once and for all; their reign is broken. But on the other hand sin and death continue to wage a rearguard and guerrilla war among the shadows; they dart out, they threaten, they are still dangerous to the unwary.

All the while, however, Christ and His soldiers are busy cleaning out the pockets of resistance; creating gardens where thistles grew or once the wreckage of battle lay strewn about; cleansing and renewing mankind, and beyond mankind, the atoms and the spiral nebulae. Though much remains to be done, and will not be fully done until Act Five, heaven has already established a firm beachhead, and the lines of communication are secure. All creation will in time be utterly and gloriously Christ's, as Christ is utterly and gloriously God's.

During this interim period, the Church is Christ's earthly body, carrying on His work. Even in the Church double sight is needed to distinguish the divine Church that is Christ's body from the all-too-human church that the camera accurately depicts. And the eyes of double sight will also detect the unofficial outposts of the Church, Christ-led and Christ-blessed, though not professedly allied with Him.

During this age of waiting and working Christ is with all who consciously or unconsciously call on His name, and though shadows everywhere weave in and out, everywhere are rumors and earnests of the ultimate light and singing; and time moves with steady pace toward its fulfillment in the fullness of time.

Act Five: The Fullness of Time. The Bible offers only the most impressionistic of hints in regard to this Act;

Christ Himself said He did not know when the curtain would go up. But He promised that no matter how long Act Four lasts, a time will come for the curtain to fall again and then rise on Act Five. When it rises, God will be revealed without disguise; it will not this time be a half-clandestine visit. At this final time God-in-Christ will come openly, and in His kingly love, to complete the remaking of all things.

Whatever and whoever will not then consent to sunlight will be given the one pocket of darkness that God will spare somewhere in the universe; we have Christ's solemn warning that those who insist on shadows will at last be granted their wish. Whatever and whoever will not join in the dance of love and sing with the exultant stars will be permitted to go into the merciful darkness, the babbling, the incoherence.

But the invitation has always been to the banquet, the dance, the singing; and it will take a very firm refusal for any stick or stone or mortal being to evade that loving invitation.

We cannot literally imagine the new world that will emerge gleaming from God's hands; how can a baby in the womb see and hear the birds that are singing in the garden? But time will be merged into the fullness of time.

When that moment—that time-transcending and time-fulfilling "now"—is fully revealed, it will not be utterly strange to us; we shall remember the glimpses we had of another land in brief moments of the opening door.

⇒≫ XXI ≪⇐

The Shape of Darkness and the Fact of Light

I BEGIN to understand many things.

Christ is God's window, through Whom we are enabled to see the red and blue and green of God's light, and not be blinded.

But Christ is more than revelation: He is salvation.

I know this, for now I begin to understand the nature of darkness. Darkness *must* shape itself into a cross. A cross is the meaning of darkness.

A cross is a crossroads. The cross of Christ is the crossroads where man's horizontal travel and God's vertical travel had to meet. The cross was not an accident. It was made of wood from the tree that Adam and Eve despoiled in Paradise.

Before I can understand God's love for me or let it fully enter, I must know how costly a love this is, and Who paid the cost.

As long as I try to earn God's love, I cannot open to it.

I look at the cross. I do not need to earn God's love. I have it already. It is there on the cross.

God loves me as I am. It remains only for me to thank Him, to love Him, and to do the works of love. And it will not be I who do them, but the Christ who is born anew in the manger of my heart.

Christ is God made man. Christ is God's light made man's light, for us men and for our salvation.

I know now what I have seen in the quick moments of the opening door, and more weakly perceived in work and thought and art and desolation and growth and everything.

I have seen the light of Christ, which is God's light.

Of His love, God has opened an occasional door, and has assailed my eyes with as much light as they can now bear.

My wounded eyes—wounded, it may be, by a maple tree in autumn foliage, or by a child singing on the way home from school—turn again to the cross.

I see it double now. Nailed to the cross is the stripped and bleeding figure, agony on the weary face.

But superimposed is another . . . a king, robed as a king. The king and the crucified are one.

Here is the light that lights all things, and it is the light by which I can hope to see.

God said, Let there be light: and there was light.

Appendix

The quotation at the beginning is from a papyrus fragment, found at Oxyrhynchus, Egypt, and believed to date from the third century A. D. I have omitted the parentheses that indicate conjectural restorations in the edition from which the quotation is cited: Montague Rhodes James, *The Apocryphal New Testament* (Clarendon Press, Oxford, 1924, page 27).

It is difficult for me to name the literary influences that have gone into the shaping of my book. Any list is certain to overlook many of them, and perhaps some of the most important. But one name is of seminal importance: C. S. Lewis. His preface to the third edition of *The Pilgrim's Regress* (Geoffrey Bles, Ltd., London, 1943) was the key I needed to make sense of those moments when the door opens and as quickly closes. He treats the same matter elsewhere, in the final chapter of *The Problem of Pain* (The Macmillan Company, New York, 1945). More recently, and in much greater detail, he has carried his exploration further with *Surprised by Joy* (Harcourt, Brace & Co., New York, 1956).

Other books that come to mind are: Martin Buber, *I and Thou*, translated by Ronald Gregor Smith (Charles Scribner's Sons, New York, 1937); F. S. C. Northrop, *The Meeting of East and West: An Inquiry Concerning World*

Understanding (The Macmillan Company, New York, 1946); Dante, *The Divine Comedy;* Charles Williams, *The Figure of Beatrice: A Study in Dante* (Faber and Faber, Ltd., London, 1943), *Descent into Hell* (Pellegrini & Cudahy, New York, 1949), *All Hallows' Eve* (Pellegrini & Cudahy, New York, 1948). All these books, in their very different fashions, illumine "the Way of the Affirmation of Images," and that is the subject of the present work.

My treatment of science—and Copernicus in particular—leans heavily on Edwin Arthur Burtt's *The Metaphysical Foundations of Modern Physical Science* (Revised edition, Doubleday & Company, Garden City, N. Y., 1954). I should like also to acknowledge with gratitude the kindness of my friend Dr. Edward C. Fuller, who checked the scientific references in my manuscript. But any errors or infelicities that remain must be distinctly debited to me.

Another good friend, Mr. Robert H. Glauber, read the manuscript and gave me invaluable criticism. Finally, I am deeply indebted to a third friend, the late John B. Chambers, one of "the scattered fellowship," whose sympathetic insight into my purposes remains a precious memory to me.

Set in Linotype Caledonia
Format by Marguerite Swanton
Manufactured by The Haddon Craftsmen, Inc.
Published by HARPER & BROTHERS, *New York*